Dr. Ruth's Guide

to

Teens
&Sex
Today

A RESOURCE FOR PARENTS

From **Social Networking** to **Friends with Benefits**

Dr. Ruth's Guide

to

Teens *Sex* Today

A RESOURCE FOR PARENTS

From **Social Networking** to **Friends with Benefits**

Dr. Ruth K. Westheimer
with Pierre A. Lehu

TEACHERS COLLEGE PRESS

Teachers College
Columbia University
New York and London

Published by Teachers College Press, 1234 Amsterdam Avenue, New York, NY 10027

Copyright © 2008 by Ruth K. Westheimer and Pierre A. Lehu

Library of Congress Cataloging-in-Publication Data

Westheimer, Ruth K. (Ruth Karola), 1928–
 Dr. Ruth's guide to teens and sex today: from social networking to friends with benefits / by Ruth K. Westheimer and Pierre A. Lehu.
    p. cm.
    Includes index.
    ISBN 978-0-8077-4905-0 (pbk.)
1. Sex instruction for teenagers. 2. Parent and teenager. 3. Teenagers—Life skills guides. I. Lehu, Pierre A. II. Title.
HQ35.W415 2008
649' .65—dc22   2008011039

ISBN: 978-0-8077-4905-0 (paper)

Printed on acid-free paper
Manufactured in the United States of America

15 14 13 12 11 10 09 08   8 7 6 5 4 3 2 1

To my children, Miriam and Joel,
with thanks for having survived their teen years.

Contents

Acknowledgments

From Dr. Ruth K. Westheimer: To the memory of my entire family who perished during the Holocaust. To the memory of my late husband, Fred, who encouraged me in all my endeavors. To my current family, my daughter Miriam Westheimer, Ed.D., son-in-law Joel Einleger, M.B.A., their children Ari and Leora, my son Joel Westheimer, Ph.D., daughter-in-law Barabara Leckie, Ph.D., and their children Michal and Benjamin. I have the best grandchildren in the entire world!

Thanks to all the many family members and friends for adding so much to my life. I'd need an entire chapter to list them all but some must be mentioned here: Pierre Lehu and I have now collaborated on fifteen books; he's the best Minister of Communications I could have asked for! Cliff Rubin, my assistant, thanks! David Best, M.D., Carlita and Tony C. de Chavez, Marcie Citron, Hersh Cohen, Martin Englisher, Elliot Horowitz, Vera Jelinek, Alfred Kaplan, Marga and Bill Kunreuther, Dean Stephen Lassonde, Rabbi and Mrs. William Lebeau, John and Ginger Lollos, Dale Ordes, Henry and Sydelle Ostberg, Commissioner Ken Podziba, Rabbi James Ponet, Fred and Anne Rosenberg, Daniel Schwartz, Amir Shaviv, Jeff Tabak, Esq., Malcolm Thomson, Greg Willenborg, and to all of the people at Teachers College Press, who worked so hard to bring this book into print, specifically Marie Ellen Larcada, Carole Saltz, and Lori Tate.

From Pierre Lehu: Thanks to my wife, Joanne Seminara, my children, Peter and Gabrielle, my daughter-in-law Melissa Sullivan, my in-laws, Joe and Anita Seminara and the entire Seminara clan. And, of course, a great big thanks to Dr. Ruth for the past 30 years of working together.

And God shall turn the heart of the parent to the child and the heart of the child to the parent

Malachi 3-24

Introduction

RAISING A CHILD these days is much different than ever before, which, in turn, makes it much more difficult. But having admitted that the task is harder for this generation than those in the past, let me start by giving you the most important piece of advice I can: don't panic. Your children, and you as parents, will get through all of this, even if you all make some mistakes. Overreacting won't make it any easier and could, in fact, make it tougher. So if there's one skill that you need to learn, it's how to take a deep breath. You'll be practicing these deep breathing techniques a lot until your children grow up and move out of the house, but your family will get through this process in one piece.

Here's another piece of advice: Don't wait to start acting like a parent. I see so many young parents these days who act as if they are their children's friends. Your children need friends their own age, and I'm sure they have plenty of them. What they need from you are parents. I don't know the age of your child, but I would advise parents to take charge as much as possible from Day One, as soon as your child comes home from the hospital. For the next 21 or so years, your child will be fighting to wrest that control from you on a daily basis, and your job will be to resist and maintain the highest level of discipline of which you're capable. In the long run you must give up control and allow your children to become responsible adults, but you want to be able to do it on your terms and as slowly as possible, because any control you give up, no matter the age of the child, will be next to impossible to get back.

What if you suddenly realize that you've given up too much control? We'll get to that later in the book, but all is not lost. The important thing is to start the process of maintaining whatever control you do have right away before you lose any more. What you must understand is that your child, be she toddler, tween, or teen, is looking for you to assert your authority as a parent. Grabbing control may seem like fun to kids of all ages, but the responsibilities that come with control can seem crushing to a child; so while a kid may complain bitterly when you lay down rules and stick to them, on the inside that child is breathing a large sigh of relief.

One last piece of general advice, before we get on with the book, is this: Become as technologically savvy as you can. When you read about the various troubles kids can get into on the Web, whether it be in this book or in newspapers or magazines, don't just throw up your hands and say, "I'll never understand any of this." On the contrary, you have a duty to become somewhat of an expert. Otherwise your kids will be able to run rings around you, and you'll have no control whatsoever over what they're doing. If kids and senior citizens can learn how to use computers, then you can too.

So the three basic rules are: don't panic, maintain control, and become an expert. By following these three basic tenets, which by the way reinforce each other, you'll be on your way to becoming the type of parent your children need in the beginning of the twenty-first century. And whenever you start to feel sorry for yourself, just give thanks that you don't have to be a parent 50 years from now when who knows what else will have been invented that will make parenting even more difficult.

A Word About Style

In the not-too-distant past, it was common for writers to use the masculine pronouns when speaking of both sexes. In today's world that is no longer acceptable, and I agree with this change heartily. But it does make it more difficult for writers, especially when the subject is sex, which clearly refers to both genders. In order not to have to keep writing "he and she" you'll note that sometimes I'll use the masculine and sometimes the feminine, though for the most part what I'm saying applies to children of both sexes. However, there is obviously advice that is appropriate for only one sex, and so at the end of each chapter I'll be breaking out relevant material that is aimed at each individual sex. In some chapters this will be more important than others, but to be consistent I'll do it in every chapter.

CHAPTER 1

The Basics

D ID YOU KNOW that little boys get erections when they're in their mother's womb and that the vaginas of little girls in the womb can become lubricated? It's true. We humans do not suddenly become sexual creatures when we hit puberty; we're born innately sexual. So while you as a parent may think that your children who haven't undergone puberty yet are asexual they're not. Obviously, younger children aren't fully developed sexually, but they're not totally oblivious to sexual feelings either. And equally important, they're also not oblivious to how you react to sex. Even if only subconsciously, they're learning about sex from you all the time. They're observing you, and it's making an impression on them, from the moment they're weeks old and can recognize your face until the day they walk out the door to go out on their own. And while I don't want you to feel self-conscious about it, you do have to take their reactions into account. You do have to monitor your behavior and make sure that you're not giving the wrong message through your actions, no matter what you are telling them verbally.

As I said in the introduction, parenting is a job that begins on Day One, when you bring your child home from the hospital. If you're very lax when it comes to discipline with young children, you're going to have a very tough time guiding them when they're teens. If they get the idea early on that they hold the reins of power, that they know best, that they can handle many aspects of life better than you can, then why should they listen to your advice, not to mention obey your commands? Part of your job as a parent making decisions is to think ahead, not just about tomorrow, but about years and even decades from today, because what you do

3

today, how you treat your children today, will have an impact all through your parenting years.

Parents Must Be Sexually Literate

Of course, for you to be able to maintain any control, you have to have a good understanding of human behavior, and with regard to the material covered in this book, that means human sexual behavior. If your sex life isn't in good shape because you have huge gaps in your knowledge, your children are going to sense that and be quite reluctant to listen to you. Therefore,while I don't want to start with a commercial for another book that I've written, I might as well use my book as an example rather than anyone else's, and so I'm suggesting you buy or borrow from your library *Sex for Dummies.*

Your Homework Assignment

There are many books that could help you become sexually literate, and maybe you even have a few on your bookshelf. So I'm not rigidly telling you to buy *Sex for Dummies.* However, it does have some advantages. For one thing, it's written in a manner that encourages you to jump around. If you think you know about the material covered in one chapter, go to another where you believe you're in need of a little education. And if you've got a teen, then maybe this will turn out to be the right book to give him or her to make sure that your teen's education is complete. I know that many parents have done exactly that, reporting that this book was perfect for giving teens a thorough overview, along with the right moral messages. But that's jumping the gun a bit. At this point I want to make sure that you know the basics and a little beyond so that if a teachable moment arises between you and a child, you won't be fumbling around for answers but will know what to say. And such moments can crop up whether the child is 2 or 20. And as I said earlier, your child will sense whether you're speaking with authority or just guessing at the answer, so it's important that you have the required knowledge and that your child knows it. (And being fully knowledgeable about sex is going to help your sex life as well, so this homework I'm giving you will pay dividends in many ways.)

Your Behavior Counts

While it takes some conscious effort to pass on sexual knowledge to your children, sexual behavior is something that is usually handed down subconsciously. Your primary reactions to sex were handed down to you by your parents, and you're passing on much of what you learned to your children. That means if your parents were prudish, you're at least somewhat prudish, though you could be very prudish, and in turn your kids will be too. On the other hand, if your parents were rather open-minded about sex, then you probably are too, and you'll pass that characteristic on to your children.

How this system of passing on values operates will depend on how aware you are of the messages you are passing on. If you don't pay attention to the messages that you're giving, then what you communicate will be your inherent characteristics. But let's say that you regret being a prude and would like to keep your children from inheriting that particular psychological trait. Because prudishness is not in your genes, but is a learned behavior, you can make changes both in your behavior and, in turn, in that of your children. Now I'm not saying that someone can simply will themselves from being prudish to becoming a nudist. You might force yourself to go to a nudist camp, but you're probably never going to feel comfortable in such surroundings, or at the very least it will take you quite a long time to adjust. And even if you did learn to feel comfortable walking around naked in front of other adults, that wouldn't mean that you'd feel equally comfortable doing the same in front of your kids. However, I'm not saying that you have to turn your personality around 180 degrees. All I'm saying is that if you recognize a weakness in your attitude toward sex, I want you to be cognizant of the fact that you're passing it on, either consciously or subconsciously, and if you're not happy with the messages you're sending, then try to make some subtle changes.

Q. I have a 16-year-old son and 14-year-old daughter, and if either
one of them sees me and my husband being at all affectionate,
they're quick to tell us to stop it. They'll say something like "Gross"
or "Act your age," and admittedly, it does inhibit us from showing
affection around them. How should we handle this situation?

A. In human society you're not supposed to have any sexual
feelings for your close relatives, and in order to make sure that
happens, we all tend to overcompensate a bit. So if you saw your
elderly neighbors giving each other a hug you might think it's cute,
but if you saw your parents hug, you might walk out of the room.
On top of that, when your kids were younger, you changed their
diapers and bathed them, and they may have watched you shower;
but now that they're more grown up, even though you still live together intimately, they are going to demand a lot more privacy for
themselves and also from being as intimate with their parents' lives
as they once were. They're in the process of separating from you,
and so it's perfectly normal that as part of that process the thought
of Mom and Dad being sexual creatures is not one that they want
to think about.

On the one hand, I would say that you should acknowledge
their feelings to some extent and not get too lovey-dovey in front
of them if it makes them feel uncomfortable, though they're always free to leave the room. On the other hand, you shouldn't
stop showing any affection for each other in their presence, both
because it sets a good example and, after all, it's your house too.
So be courteous of their feelings, and refrain from acting too physically amorous, but continue to show each other affection so that
you don't do any damage to your relationship, as the two of you
can't limit your signs of affection for each other to occur only behind closed bedroom doors.

Fighting Peer Pressure

Why should you change your attitudes about sex just for your
children's sake? Your authority over your children is not absolute,
as there are other forces out there trying to stage a coup d'etat
against you, the main one being peer pressure. Very few children

can stand up to peer pressure 100% of the time. That means if you're saying no to everything that peer pressure is telling your child he or she must do to be cool, you're going to lose many of those battles, and more important, you won't know which ones. If you can pick and choose your battles, then you'll stand a better chance of maintaining some control.

I'll have more to say about peer pressure in Chapter 4. But let me explain the point I'm making here, using oral sex as an example: If you think oral sex is disgusting but peer pressure is instructing your children that it's acceptable, then you'll have difficulties communicating with your child on this subject. You may have more of an effect on your teen's behavior if you obtain a better understanding of oral sex in our society rather than rejecting it out of hand. Adopting a more flexible attitude will permit more open communications between you and your teen, both on the conscious and unconscious level, allowing you to have more influence over your teen than you would if your mind was totally closed to such concepts as oral sex.

Fear Doesn't Work Either

When American troops were being sent overseas to fight in the two world wars, they were shown films depicting all the horrible things that could happen to them if they went to a prostitute and caught a sexually transmitted disease (STD). They were shown pictures of penises that were covered with sores or dripping with pus. Certainly, the men left the screenings of those films vowing to stay away from any prostitutes they might encounter, but the fact is the prostitutes ended up being just as busy as they would have been had the soldiers not been shown those films. Sexual urges are very strong, and after a time of being away from home, when confronted with the opportunity of having sex with a prostitute, the troops forgot all about the films they had been shown. The risks, which might have seemed grave during their training, became trivial when they were faced with the temptation of having sex with a prostitute when they were so far from home during a dangerous war. It would have been better from the health-related point of view of preventing the spread of STDs, if the army had recognized the impossibility of stopping the troops from going to prostitutes simply by trying to scare them and instead had provided them with information about the risks and with condoms to protect themselves.

Teens tend to believe they're immortal. They're not as worried about the consequences of their actions as adults are. But that's not entirely their fault. Because we tend to infantilize our teens, telling them what they can't do more often than forcing them to be responsible for their actions, they don't have a good appreciation of the consequences of those actions. As a result, telling teens, who are used to being treated like children, that they shouldn't have sex because they might catch a disease or cause an unintended pregnancy isn't as effective as it could be. In their minds, if they run into a jam, they can always turn to Mom and Dad to help them out of it, and so they're just not as concerned about risks as they should be. Rather than just saying no, what parents have to do is to make sure that their teens understand as much about sex as possible, both the good and the bad, and also understand that they will have to face the consequences of their actions. Armed with knowledge and the right overall upbringing, most teens will act responsibly.

Ducking the Issue

Of course that's the harder way. It's easier to just say no because then you don't have to have a series of talks with your teens about sex. Since so many of us feel quite uncomfortable talking about sex, especially with our own children, by saying no to teen sex, we may feel we've done our part. But if that "no" is not likely to be obeyed, then we might as well not have said a word.

To illustrate what I'm saying, let me compare sex with driving. Most parents don't try to stop their teens from learning how to drive; in fact, most parents spend a lot of time taking their kids out on the road to let them practice, in addition to making sure that they take driver's ed in school. Here's a case where everyone is on the same page. The teens want to learn how to drive and their parents do all they can to make sure they drive as safely as possible.

How many parents take the same path when it comes to sex? How many parents sit down with their kids and say, "Yes, I know you want to learn how to have sex so I'm going to teach you everything I know about sex so that you can have sex safely"? Those parents are few and far apart. And yet every parent knows that their kids are sexual beings and will be having sex some day, and maybe sooner than later. So why doesn't every parent adopt the same attitude with sex as they do with driving?

I admit there are other factors involved, like religious beliefs and family values, but the situation is even more complicated than that because most parents are giving their teens two messages: (1) Wait until you're married to have sex, and (2) don't get married too soon. Considering how strong the urge to have sex is, that is a formula for failure. If you want your child to go to college and you're telling that child not to get married before graduation, that means you're saying not to get married until this young adult is at least 21. But it's during the teen years that a human's sexual hormones are surging at their highest level. At no time in our lives do we have a stronger desire to have sex than the very years parents are telling their children not to have sex and not to get married. How any parent can be surprised that their child is disobeying this ridiculous set of rules is beyond me. In fact, statistics show that most teens do become sexually active long before they get married. So while I'm not suggesting you tell your teens to go out and have sex, I am advising you not to stick your head in the sand and pretend that they're going to abstain just because you've instructed them to do so.

An Alternate Model

One reason that parents don't want their teens having sex are the inherent risks. Yes, there were dangers when they were riding their bikes too, but any parent looking at the statistics for unintended pregnancies and the spread of sexually transmitted diseases is understandably going to be a little panicky at the thought of their child becoming sexually active. Is there any hope for teens to behave more responsibly? If you take a look at another model, European teens, I think that you'll feel relieved to know that there is hope.

European parents might be happier if their children were getting married earlier, but they're realistic enough to understand that married or not, their teens are going to be having sex. So the message most European parents are telling their offspring is that it's

OK to have sex without marriage, but only if they're in a serious relationship. And with this limited approval, they're also telling them how to have responsible sex. And the result is that European young people are having fewer unintended pregnancies and fewer abortions. (According to a recent study, the American rate of abortions is 21 per 100 pregnancies while in Europe it's 13.)* So the reality is that the American model leads to more abortions, even though American parents tend to be against abortion in much greater numbers than European parents.

The Wisdom of the Ages

Throughout mankind's history and continuing today in many parts of the world, parents arrange for their children to be married as soon as they are physically ready. The wisdom of the ages was that you couldn't stop young people from having sex, so if you didn't want to have a lot of illegitimate children running around, you made sure that your children got married as soon as they were ready to make children. With the advent of widespread birth control, this model no longer has to be followed to prevent illegitimate births, but then some other model needs to be put into place. At the moment, that new model seems to be in a state of flux, as parents can't figure out what the best course of action might be. While I might not be able to give you a detailed road map for your family, I at least want you to have a better understanding of all the factors at play here so that you can make the best decision. And if your current plan is either to ignore your children's sexuality or push only abstinence, then my goal is to steer you in a new direction.

A Word About Privacy

I am very much in favor of privacy. I think parents should knock on their children's door before entering, so that if they're masturbating they can hide the evidence, and I believe that children should also knock, so that parents can have the privacy they

*Henshaw, S. K., Singh, S., & Haas, T. (1999). The incidence of abortion worldwide, family planning perspectives, Vol. 25: http://www.guttmacher.org/pubs/journals/25s3099.html.

need to have their own sex life. (A lock on the parental bedroom door would also be helpful.) I also extend that right to privacy in the arena of sex to partners in a relationship: I don't think that you need to tell a partner all about your past lovers. You don't have to lie and say you were a virgin, but you don't have to paint a vivid picture either.

Getting back to the subject at hand, while I want you parents to make certain that your children know all they need to know about the mechanics of sex, I don't believe that you have to be best friends and talk about what they're actually doing sexually. Your job isn't to tell them what positions to use, but instead to make sure that they're as safe as possible. You have to retain your role as parent, and to do that requires some separation. And they have to grow up and learn to stand on their own, which is another reason for the need of separation. Yes, they should feel that they can approach you if they run into trouble, and can ask you questions if they need information, but when the subject is sex, it's not like you're the coach of their little league team and should be the one to explain to them how to stand when waiting for a pitch. I think discussing the benefits of different sex positions with your children is carrying things too far. If one of your children asks you a very specific question, certainly you should answer it if you can, but I don't believe such discussions should be initiated by a parent. At some point, you might be needed to fill your role as parent, putting your foot down about one thing or another, and if you've become too much like friends, that's not going to work. (There will come a time when they're truly adults and then your relationship might change, but that's beyond the scope of this book.)

There's a term that was coined by another sex educator, which is *askable parent.*[†] I definitely want you to be one of those, someone whom your child, whatever his age, feels can be approached and asked any type of question. Nevertheless, an askable parent is still first of all a parent, so be careful not to allow the relationship to get so close that you feel uncomfortable being a figure of authority as well as one who gives advice.

And while I am encouraging you to give your child as much

---

† This term was created by Sol Gordon and Judith Gordon in their book, *Raising a Child Responsibily in a Sexually Permissive World* (Holbrook MA: Adams Media).

privacy as makes sense, I recognize there may be times when in your role as parent you are going to have to pry. If you sense that your child is doing something dangerous, then you have a right to interfere. Of course making that decision, whether to invade the child's privacy or not, is rarely an easy one. For example, if you have a teenage daughter whom you believe may be sexually active, you may want her to see an ob-gyn in order to get a prescription for the pill. Protecting her from an unintended pregnancy is the responsible thing to do. In order to get her to go, you may have to ask her whether or not she's having intercourse. She could "only" be having oral sex, in which case there'd be no need for her to be on the pill (unless she was about to "graduate" from oral sex to intercourse), but having a discussion about her sexual activities while at the same time allowing her to keep her privacy is going to require careful navigation. I'll discuss this topic in greater depth later in this book, but I didn't want to leave you with the impression that I was against a parent doing any prying, because that's not the case. The point I want to make is that invading your child's privacy is not something to do lightly, but if it has to be done, then so be it.

Improving Your Own Sex Life

As I said earlier, children receive messages from their parents whether or not they're intended. If your sex life is far from what it could be, then how this affects your attitude toward sex is going to be somewhat evident. If you're not having sex, then you're probably not hugging and kissing in front of your children. So the message to your children is that their parents are cold, not loving and warm. If that's the example a child has been given, to some extent that lifestyle is the one that's going to be expected. If your son or daughter is in a relationship with a partner who doesn't show much affection, even though your child wants to be kissed and hugged, your child is going to think that it's normal not to receive affection. Rather than moving on to someone else, your son or daughter will stick it out, not realizing that a couple are supposed to act lovingly toward one another. So any negatives in your sex life, even though you think you're keeping them private, could have a negative impact on your children. Obviously, you should want to fix up any negative areas in your sex life just because you want to have as positive a sex life as possible; but another reason to make sure that your overall relationship, not just your sex life, is as good as it can be in the example it sets for your children.

How to make those improvements is not in the scope of this book, but I do want to encourage you to consider taking some action, if you believe you need to, either by reading up on the subject or consulting with a therapist.

Teamwork

There's still another reason why I want your relationship to be in good shape, and that's because effective parenting means that both parents are working together to raise their kids, not working at cross-purposes. For that to happen, sometimes one parent has to compromise. If the two parents are on good terms, working out such compromises is not too difficult. But if the parents' relationship is severely frayed, then negotiating a compromise could be quite difficult.

Why is it important that you are both on the same page when making decisions about your children? The reason is that if you're working at cross-purposes, your children will sense that and use it against both of you. If the kids know that Mom will say no, they'll go to Dad if they think he'll say yes. In the end, the kids will get their way, which is rarely the best way.

This situation can be especially difficult if parents are divorced. In this case the relationship has already collapsed, and far too often one or both parents take the fight into the arena of parenting. While I understand how tempting this can be because you can really hurt someone by manipulating parent/child relationships, the ones who suffer are the children. If you're in such a situation, the best course to follow is to give in. Unless your former spouse is crazy, and would allow your child to engage in self-destructive behavior just because he or she knows how much it would hurt you, it's better to act as one with regard to your children than to divide yourselves, which really offers the children no guidance whatsoever.

Girls and Boys

At the start of this chapter I wrote about the passing of your values on to your children. Among those values some are sex specific. In other words, you want to make sure that your male offspring develop the right attitude about females, and vice versa. In order to take this into account, I will consider boys and girls separately and at the end of each chapter give appropriate advice for each gender.

For Boys

I don't keep up with the music scene all that closely, but I'm hoping that as I write this that we are coming to the end of the hip-hop era, or at least the part of it that is misogynist. No matter what you want to teach your male children about how they should treat females, the job is that much harder when they are hearing lyrics that demean women. You could try banning those songs in your household, but in today's world, music isn't stored on discs any more, which are easy to check, but rather in portable devices that often contain literally thousands of songs. For a parent to try to keep watch over what the iPod generation is listening to is almost impossible. Besides that, even if this music isn't in your house, a teen is likely going to hear it outside of the home environment.
So what you as a parent must do is sit down and talk with your son about respecting women. I know that the first words out of his mouth are going to be, "But I don't take that seriously, it's just music." You have to explain to him that while that is perhaps true on a conscious level, listening to such lyrics over and over again will have a subconscious effect.

We all know that having one talk is not going to be enough. What I recommend to you is that whenever you get a chance to show your son the full value of women, you do so. For example, if there is a woman candidate running for office, whether you agree with her political views, don't allow comments in your house that indicate that she shouldn't get elected because she's a woman. If there's a news story about a woman who has made a significant accomplishment, make your son read it. In other words, be proactive about this campaign. And when your son starts dating, have a talk with him and see how he feels about the young lady he's seeing. If he offers any indication that he doesn't have full respect for her, then speak up and let him know that his attitude is not acceptable.

For Girls

Women seem to have more self-esteem issues than men. In part, it's because our society puts so much importance on their appearance. And while older men may have learned to respect women more, that's not necessarily true of younger men, in part because they're not entirely sure of themselves and gravitate toward the idea that by putting down women they are elevating themselves.

As a parent of a daughter, you must do what you can to counteract this effect. Your daughter needs to hear from you that she is valued, and if you have a male child, that she is valued as much as your son. Traditionally the son was always given the favored position in the family. If that attitude existed in your home when you were growing up, then you can assume that some of this tradition will survive in your attitude toward your daughter. What you must do is watch what you say in front of her and make an effort to build her ego up as much as possible. Maybe one day this won't be required, but today it most certainly is.

CHAPTER 2

Your Child's Changing Body

FROM THE MOMENT they are born, children are constantly growing and changing. Some changes are simple to adapt to, like getting taller and losing their baby teeth, though buying new clothes and sending them to the orthodontist can be expensive. But sexual changes are another story: They signify that your child is becoming an adult, usually far earlier than you want this to occur. These changes also bring with them a new set of dangers, like the risk of catching a sexually transmitted disease or undergoing an unintended pregnancy, which are in a different category than scraped knees and mosquito bites. But most important, these physical changes will signify a change in your relationship with your children. They will no longer be "your little boy or girl" but will demand independence. So these physical changes need to be respected, not just for what they will do to your child's body, but what they mean for your child in so many other ways.

Secondary Sexual Characteristics

These changes fall into the category of what are called *secondary sexual characteristics*. In both sexes, they include new hair growth—on arms, underarms, legs, and in the pubic area—changes in body odor, and very often changes in complexion (i.e., pimples). For girls, breasts will develop, their hips will get wider, their vaginas will develop, and they will begin to menstruate. For boys, their muscles will grow stronger, their voices will deepen, they'll grow facial hair, and their penises will grow, have erections, and produce nocturnal emissions.

Exactly when these changes take place depends on the individual child, as well as on the sex of the child, with girls beginning earlier than boys. Some children can begin noticing such changes as young as 7 or 8 (though 10 is a more common age for these changes to begin), while other children don't fully develop until they are as old as 16. And it's a gradual process, so your daughter, for example, won't grow breasts overnight, but will slowly form them over a period of a year or two.

As a matter of interest, for reasons that are unknown the age that children reach puberty has been getting younger. Between 1860 and 1960 the age at which females reached puberty declined by about 3 months per decade to about 12.5 years of age for females and about 14 years for males.‡ This is one reason that parenting has become harder, because younger children may not be as ready for these changes.

Precocious Puberty

Some children undergo what is called *precocious puberty;* that is to say, they show some signs of puberty much earlier than they should. There are two aspects to this condition, the psychological and the physical. I talk about how it feels to be the first in your group to reach puberty later on, but when it happens to a very young child, then the psychological issues are more serious. And because reaching the end of puberty is a signal for the body to stop growing, young children who enter puberty too early may never reach their full height potential. So if your child either exhibits these changes earlier than you'd expect or doesn't develop them by the age of sixteen, consult your physician.

Raging Hormones

Obviously, such fundamental changes affect children more than the normal growth spurt—and that's just the visible changes.

‡ Tanner, J.M. (1978). *Foetus into man: Physical growth from conception to maturity.* Cambridge: Harvard University Press.

Reaching puberty means that the sex glands have matured and are now releasing all sorts of hormones into your child's bloodstream, which are having psychological effects as well as physical ones. So if a postpubescent child seems extra moody, there may well be a chemical reason for it. This means that reason may go out the window now and then, and your child will react emotionally rather than rationally. Sorry, but that's all in a day of growing up with a teen.

Timing

These changes will also affect children differently depending on when they occur. Children tend to be grouped according to age in school, and so in every class there is going to be one person who starts changing first, as well as a few who will hang back. Each will face a different set of problems.

A girl who begins to develop breasts before any other girl in the class, or a boy who is the first to sprout facial hair, may be made fun of until a few others catch up. Usually it doesn't take long for some others to start undergoing these changes, and it's the laggards who end up feeling bad. Many girls ask for "training bras" before there's anything to train. Where boys may find it difficult is in gym class if they have to shower. To be the last one without pubic hair is certainly embarrassing, but there's nothing that can be done; if the waiting period drags on too long, then a doctor should be consulted.

While a parent may not be able to do anything for a child who is off schedule from a medical point of view, giving psychological support can be very important so that the child does not develop body image issues. Your job as the parent of a child who is developing either very early or very late is to be as supportive as possible with regard to every other aspect of the child's life aside from physical appearance. Be quick to praise your child for success in school or at athletics. If your child seems moody, try to find ways of elevating his or her spirits. Even if your offers are rejected, which may be a part of that moodiness, your child still needs to hear your encouragement. Although it can be difficult for you as parent, remember that it's even more difficult for your child and do the best you can to support your girl or boy during this trouble-some period.

Dealing with a Child of the Opposite Sex

All parents have gone through puberty and so know to some extent what to expect with regard to their own sex, though your viewpoint of those times was certainly colored by your own mood-iness. But when it comes to dealing with a child of the opposite sex, then you won't have that personal experience to fall back on, which is why I want to point out the potential pitfalls to these changes.

Nocturnal Emissions

The first one I'd like to bring up is nocturnal emissions, or "wet dreams." What happens is that a boy wakes up to discover that he ejaculated during REM sleep. If it just occurred, he'll open his eyes and his first reaction may be "That was pleasant," but then he'll realize that his pajamas are full of this gooey white stuff, which is quite an unpleasant experience. And no matter how hard he tries to clean it up, there will be a residue either on his pajamas, under-pants, sheets, or all three.

While a boy's father shared the same experiences (and may still share them, as some grown men continue to have wet dreams), to many mothers, at least when it comes to their firstborn sons, this residue may come as a surprise. Many mothers make the mistake of scolding their boys for the mess, maybe even accusing them of having urinated. The young men, of course, have absolutely no control over these wet dreams, would gladly prevent them if they could, and are probably ashamed, and so they won't give a cogent answer to such an accusation.

Since they are not in the boy's control, there's not a whole lot that you can say about wet dreams, other than to explain what they are and assure your son that they are a perfectly normal re-action to growing up so he should not get upset after having one. You could establish some rules about the cleanup of wet dreams, because an immediate sponging off will be more effective than if the residue sits around for a long time. Making sure a box of tissues is always by your son's bed would be a good proactive measure. I certainly wouldn't recommend mentioning it every time you find stained underwear or pajamas in the laundry. It is an embarrassing event for him, and there's no point rubbing it in since it is unavoidable.

Because it happens with slightly more frequency to boys who do not masturbate (as discovered by sex researcher Alfred Kinsey), masturbation may be a way of limiting the occurrence of nocturnal emissions, but there is no proof of that, and so no need to tell your child that he should start masturbating to limit the amount of wet dreams he has. On the other hand, as I said earlier, it's important to give your child the privacy he needs to masturbate, which helps to relieve sexual tensions, as well as potentially prevent wet dreams.

Not every boy will wake up because of a wet dream (which means cleanup will be that much harder later on, but again, this is not under his control) and not every wet dream is accompanied by an orgasm. Apparently sometimes the fluid just leaks out.

Females, too, can have orgasms in their sleep, but since those aren't accompanied by any physical evidence, they rarely come up in conversation with your children. However, if a daughter asks you about it, just let her know that there's nothing to worry about and that such dreams are perfectly normal. Since fewer females masturbate than males, such orgasms may be the first ones that your daughter may experience. If she says anything, tell her that the pleasure from orgasms is not anything to feel guilty about and that it is a good sign that she can have orgasms.

Menarche

Menarche is the term used for a woman's first period. For a young girl, it's an important milestone about a bodily function that will affect her monthly for the next few decades. Your daughter should certainly know to expect this long before it might actually occur. You don't want her worried to death the first time she discovers that she's bleeding from her vagina. You want her to be as informed as possible and to have the lines of communication open so that she'll come to you for assistance. A good opportunity to have such a discussion is after a shopping trip where her mom has bought pads or some other product to absorb the blood. For a daughter to know that her mother undergoes this experience monthly will ease her fears a great deal.

> Q. When I was 12, my mother had a talk with me and gave me a box of pads, which I know she used. I didn't switch to using tampons until I went to college. My daughter is at the age when I have to have the same talk. She's only seen me buy tampons, but I don't know if it's an option I should start her with or whether she should begin with pads.

A. It might be easier to use pads at first, as there isn't much of a learning curve. Many girls start out having irregular periods, so the final decision does not have to be made right away, but can wait for a while. But I think ultimately the choice should be hers. Explain to her about both products and let her decide which she wants to use. Definitely tell her that most girls won't break their hymen using tampons, and if she has problems in the beginning, she can apply a lubricant to make it easier. If she's starting to menstruate, then it's time she saw a gynecologist, some of whom report that girls who use tampons have an easier time when it comes to a gynecological exam. But the bottom line is that it is her body, and so other than supplying her with information, the answers to her questions, and the actual product, you should allow her to decide for herself.

Some women have worse periods than others, which are either preceded by mood swings or accompanied by severe cramps. If you're a woman who has such problems, and your daughter knows it, then you have to make sure that you explain to your daughter that this is not something that will definitely happen to her, though it could. She's going to be frightened enough until she actually experiences her first few periods, so there's no reason to make her any more alarmed.

Fathers and Daughters

In general it is a daughter's mother who will handle the issue of menstruation, which is logical since she's the one with the most experience. But here I want to make an important point about an area that affects fathers and daughters. Today, most fathers are involved with the raising of their children, and so it's not at all unusual to have the children come into very close contact with their daddy, with lots of hugs and kisses. When a young girl starts turning into a woman, however, some dads back off from physical contact. They're afraid of becoming physically aroused from cuddling with their daughter, who now has breasts and a developing body. While they may give her a quick peck now and then, actual physical signs of affection become taboo.

While there is some logic to this from the father's point of view, I want you to look at it from the daughter's perspective. Suddenly her dad, with whom she had been physically close, no longer wants to go near her. He won't let her sit on his lap or put his arms around her to give her a big hug. She will never figure out the real reason, so she's left to deduce why her father is now rejecting her, and she'll probably blame herself. It could cause her self-esteem to plummet. Also she will definitely miss this affection, and it could lead her to seek a replacement, so that she'll find herself with a serious boyfriend long before she would have entered into such a relationship had she remained physically close with her dad. And on top of that, she'll be more vulnerable to this young boy's advances, not wanting to be rejected by a second important male in her life.

The answer, obviously, is for dads not to push their daughters away. If it makes you a little uncomfortable to be so physically close to your daughter, all I can say is to do the best you can. Don't worry about becoming excited, because you probably won't. So your daughter's breasts are pushed up against you; for once in your life you're going to have to forget that breasts are sex objects and think of them just as mammary glands. I know that you can get over any embarrassment, especially when you realize the negative effects on your daughter that would come from pushing her away.

Confusion Reigns

If you think that you're a bit confused about how to handle your newborn teenager, just imagine how confusing it is to go through all these changes. Of course you went through them too, but no matter how much you remember of this period, it's a difficult one. And if it appears that your teen is getting through it without a hitch, rather than accept that outward appearance, look a little deeper. This stage of life is difficult, and if a teen is hiding the difficulties, then that might be a sign of something more serious taking place. If your teen is acting moody and suddenly demanding privacy and you're at odds with your child over this and that, then you can be certain that everything is normal. But if your teen is showing no signs of change, then you may want to find out why. It may be too good to be true.

No matter how rough things may become around your house as your child enters the teenage years, the most important thing to remember is that it won't last forever. At some point your teen's hormones will get into balance and your relationship will stabilize. Until then, make sure you're there to offer help, and just fasten your seat belts!

For Boys

I spoke earlier of the embarrassment that a tween or teen boy might feel, especially in the locker room, if he's among the last of his group to develop the secondary sexual characteristics, such as pubic hair. Even after a boy has gone through puberty, many young males still have locker-room problems because of the size of their penis. Now I'm famous for saying that penis size doesn't matter in the bedroom, but I doubt that most teenage boys have heard this message. And in all probability your son hasn't seen his father's penis very often, if at all, and most definitely not when it is erect, so he has very little evidence to judge his penis by. I am certainly not advocating that fathers go around showing their sons their penis. But I do think that it might be an appropriate subject of conversation.

The assumption that you're making is that your son is concerned about the size of his penis, both in its flaccid and erect state. How do you get the message across that your son's penis is normal, especially if you haven't seen it for quite some time? I would suggest starting with some questions about what goes on in his locker room. Do the boys shower? Or before engaging in sports, are they forced to put on a jock strap, which would mean removing their underwear in front of the other boys. If the answer is yes, then Dad just has to say a few words such as, "Yes, it's an embarrassing situation, but everyone feels embarrassed, and most men have the feeling that their penis doesn't measure up, but in the end women need a man skilled in the art of love, not one with a big penis. In other words, don't sweat it." Will it give him total confidence the next time he's walking around the locker room naked? No, but it may make him feel a little better, and at this point, until he's proven himself a successful lover, that's about all you can hope for.

For Girls

Being a teenager often means having some problems with your appearance. A girl just entering her teen years may still have some baby fat, she may have pimples, she may need braces; in other words she may not be all that attractive, but that doesn't mean that she won't be very attractive in a few years. Boys go through the same changes, but boys are nowhere near as concerned with their appearance as are girls. Usually being good at sports or video games concerns them more. But teenage girls are very conscious of each other's appearance, and your daughter may be having difficulties as she goes through this awkward stage.

While she may appear to shrug off compliments given to her by her parents and grandparents, don't let yourself be fooled by that seeming indifference. Such compliments will have an impact and so are very important. Dads and granddads have to be part of this process too, because if she's not getting any compliments from any male family members, she won't have as much faith in those coming from the females.

CHAPTER 3

Talking About
the Birds and the Bees

AVING ORGASMS IN your sleep and growing breasts are strange phenomena, especially if you're just coming out of childhood. Any young person is going to worry about all these changes, so it is your job as a parent to make sure that your teen, or soon-to-be teen, knows about them ahead of time so that they'll have an easier time dealing with these worries. In sitcoms, that's the time for the birds and the bees talk, but in real life I don't think that one formal session is necessarily the best way to handle this situation. First of all, since you're not an expert at speaking about sex, you're likely to become embarrassed. So will your teen. If you're both embarrassed, how much information is actually going to be passed on? Not much, I'm afraid. Even if you managed to stammer out a full explanation of wet dreams, for example, how much of the information would be retained by your child, especially if it's part of a larger dialogue that includes such topics as intercourse and contraception. As I said before, you have to be an askable parent—your child has to know that he can ask you questions if he's confused—but as to all the material that needs to be covered, I'd recommend that the bulk of the information be given via an age-appropriate book rather than a 30-minute or even an hour lecture. Then you can answer any further questions, knowing that the basics have been covered.

There are several advantages to this method of instruction. For one thing, it will be age appropriate. If you're talking to an 11-year-old you're going to want to give different information than to a 16-year-old. In the heat of a conversation, you might take a topic too far. But if you spend time looking through the books that are available, you'll certainly find one that will have the right information for your child's age. If your child then asks you more detailed questions, you can give her the answers she seeks. As your child gets older, you can give her a new book that will contain more details.

The other advantage of a book is that your tween or teen can look at it in private. That will give your child the opportunity to digest the material and maybe link it to her own life. Your child can read a few pages, and if she needs time to think, the book can be set aside and then picked up again later. If you're wondering whether your child has read the book, ask some questions that will help you determine whether the book has been actually read. If your child hasn't hit puberty yet, perhaps she won't be ready to absorb this information, and that's OK as long as the child isn't old enough to be at risk. When it comes to slightly older children, most tweens or teens are going to examine the contents of the book, I would even say rather closely. With kids that age, the curiosity level about sex is quite high, whether or not they've ever let that fact out to you.

Once you're convinced that your child knows the basics because she's read the book, then you can sit her down to address particular issues, knowing that you don't have to start at the beginning. Just because I'm telling you to begin the process with a book, let me stress that it's important to actually talk to your children about sex. If you never instigate such conversations, then your child is going to assume that you're not an askable parent, that you'd prefer to stay away from the topic of sex. But if you can pick and choose your subject matter, then the process of conveying all the information that your daughter needs to know will be much easier. For example, if you read an article about birth control in the paper, you can tell your teen to read it and then have a discussion about it. The whole process might take only 15 minutes, but not only will it give you the chance to get some of your opinions across, but you'll also be better able to gauge your child's overall knowledge by her responses. Having such conversations regularly will end up being a lot more productive than trying to cram everything into one long birds-and-bees-type lecture.

When the Subject Gets More Personal

Q. I'm a 42-year-old mother of three children. My 14-year-old son was in the bathroom when he got a phone call from a friend. I went in there a few minutes later and discovered a copy of *Playboy*, which in his rush to get to the phone he'd obviously left behind. Since I didn't want his little sister to see it, I took it, and not knowing what to do with it, I threw it in the trash. We never discussed the incident. Should I have? Or should I have told his father to talk to him about it?

A. You may not have talked to him, but that doesn't mean you didn't communicate. At some point after he got off the phone, he must have realized that he'd left the magazine behind and went back to get it; when he found it missing, he then knew you took it but didn't say anything about it. What messages did you send him? One, that you know he masturbates. Two, that you don't disapprove too much or else you would have said something. But since you didn't return the magazine, you obviously don't approve either.

Basically, I would say these messages are benign. If you had felt comfortable returning the magazine and saying, "It's OK for you to masturbate in the bathroom, but just don't leave a magazine like this around because of your younger sister," then that would have been a bit better. But if you were too embarrassed, there was no need to do more than you did. However, while masturbation isn't harmful, other aspects of his sex life could be. So if you're embarrassed talking about sex, rather than push an incident such as this under the rug, use it as an incentive to force yourself to do whatever you can to make sure that your son does understand as much as he can understand about sex at this point in his life. If all you can manage is to blurt out, "I want to make sure that you don't do anything stupid so read this book," while handing him a book on sex, then that's not so terrible. Your son deserves some privacy with regard to his sex life, as do you, but don't allow your embarrassment to keep you from at least making sure that he's protected by a minimal level of sexual literacy.

Exactly how you handle the birds and bees talk will be somewhat up to you and your child. Some children will want to have this discussion with you and some won't. Some will come to you with questions and some won't. To my way of thinking, this situation is a little like when I give a lecture. I always ask if there is anyone in the audience who wants to ask a question. Invariably, there are people with questions, but usually those questions are pretty tame. I can almost predict what they will be. (That's not so with college audiences any more. Now there are always a few students who want to prove how daring they are by asking Dr. Ruth a question that will make even her blush!) But I also always ask that cards be handed out to the audience for writing questions on, and those questions are usually much more interesting. That's because sex is somewhat embarrassing to talk about, but since so many people have huge gaps in their knowledge, it's important that the information gets out, no matter what it takes to make that happen. So don't count on getting asked an embarrassing question, and don't breathe a sigh of relief if you never get asked one either. Your job is to make sure that your children understand as much about sex as they can, both so that they can fully enjoy it and so that they are protected against the potentially dangerous consequences. It's up to you to take the initiative. If you think it's time to educate your child, then make sure that he's been given a book, and after some time has passed, say a week or so, sit him down and start a conversation that will give you the assurance that the information you want him to have has been adequately digested.

The School Yard

If you don't take care of educating your child about sex, she's going to find out some information from her friends. Some may be correct, and some will most certainly not be. You don't want your child's only source of information to be the rumors passed around in the school yard. Therefore, it's up to you to make sure that the proper information gets into your child's hands one way or another, because sooner or later your child will become sexually active and will need that information. That day is not in your control, but making sure that your teen understands the basics is.

The Talk

Now we're in agreement that you and your child are going to talk about sex. Part of the reason is so that you can ascertain how much he already knows and so that you can correct any misinformation. You also want to make sure that he's learned not only how to have sex but how to have safe sex.

Since I know this is difficult for every parent, I want to give you some advice, some of which is based on experience from before I was "Dr. Ruth." Several of the friends of my children came to me to get their questions answered long before I had a radio show, so not only did I handle this task for my own children, but it seems that I did a good enough job at it that the word spread that I was the askable parent for friends as well.

To begin, I need to put some things on the table. The first is that your sex life is off limits. Some kids will try to push the envelope, but you must say that this is private. Now it means that you also must extend this privacy to your own children. You may know if a son is having wet dreams, but you needn't know whether or not he is masturbating. Since your children will want to maintain their privacy, you shouldn't have a hard time getting them to agree to leave your privacy intact too. (Incidentally, setting this precedent with regard to sex may serve you well when talking about alcohol and drugs during some other conversation. Teens will often ask whether you used drugs or how much you drank as a teen. If you've established the concept that your life is private, then you won't be pushed into a corner on these other issues.)

But while I don't encourage you to ask a teenager whether he or she is sexually active, at the same time you have to make very clear that just because you're telling a young person about contraceptives does not mean that you are giving them your permission to be sexually active. Obviously, making that decision requires that a person know as much as possible about sex, including how to prevent pregnancy and disease, but that knowledge alone isn't enough to make the decision. Such a decision requires a lot of other factors including the strength of the relationship, the maturity of the people involved, and the ability to deal with an accident, because intercourse can have consequences even if protection is used. So you have a duty to accompany all the facts with a lesson on values that affect how those facts are to be used.

Oral and Anal Sex

These days, many teens are engaging in other forms of sex besides intercourse, including heavy petting, oral sex, and anal sex. These acts do not pose any risks with regard to an unintended pregnancy, but certain diseases, such as herpes, can still be passed on in these ways, and that message must be conveyed. Now to some of us older folk, the idea of protecting one's virginity by engaging in oral and anal sex seems quite strange. But if something like oral sex has become the norm these days, then rather than simply being outraged, you have to accept the possibility that your child is taking part in one of these activities. You should be aware that oral sex is something that younger and younger teens, and even tweens, are doing. According to the Centers for Disease Control and Prevention, more than half of all teenagers over the age of 15 are having oral sex. And what's worse (from my point of view) is that these teens aren't just having oral sex with someone with whom they're in a relationship, but many engage in this activity rather cavalierly with friends, or even people they barely know. Sharing each other's genitals has become like sharing a cigarette, drink, or joint in some circles.

This casual attitude is quite worrisome because it will shape their future serious relationships, and I'm afraid not in a good way. A serious relationship or marriage needs intimacy to be part of its foundation, but when young people are performing intimate acts outside of the bounds of an intimate relationship, what will there be left for them to use as the glue to hold together their future long-term relationships? While we can't be certain of the effects, I would predict that the relationships these young people form are going to be at greater risk. Explaining about this category of risk stemming from sex therefore becomes important. A teen would never recognize such a danger on his or her own because without the experience of being in a long-term relationship, no one can fully understand what it takes to hold one together. But I believe the logic will become apparent once you point it out to your teen.

Whether or not that will be enough to change your teen's behavior is another story.

Another concern I have about oral sex is that among these teenagers, it may mean mostly fellatio, or "blow jobs," rather than cunnilingus; in other words, it's something that girls are doing for boys but not the other way around. To some extent, I believe that many girls were masturbating their boyfriends without getting orgasms in return long before oral sex became as prevalent as it is. But masturbation doesn't entail any physical risks, while oral sex docs. For example, doctors are seeing more and more cases of oral herpes on people's genitals, and vice versa. And let's face it, putting a penis into your mouth increases the level of intimacy considerably.

The problem for parents is that if you say to a young girl, "It's one thing to masturbate a boyfriend but quite another to give him oral sex," I believe that peer pressure is going to weigh more heavily than your words. If a girl hears from other girls that they are giving blow jobs to their boyfriends, then she's much more likely to give in when she's asked, whether it turns your stomach or not. So what's your best course of action?

I think you have to give two messages. The first is purely sexual: Use condoms. Make sure that your daughter knows that she can catch a disease from oral sex, so even though she can't become pregnant, she must use condoms for intercourse, oral sex, and anal sex. That's not an easy message to give, and you will certainly be thinking long and hard exactly how you are going to phrase it, but if you do a good job, you may actually exert enough pressure to make your daughter at least delay the stage of giving oral sex as she is forced to consider the risks.

The second message is that she is as deserving of pleasure as a young man: Sex is not something that you do for somebody else, but that two people do for each other. In addition, it should only be part of a relationship, not done just in passing. Now this message has to be part of a bigger message about being treated equally as a woman. That's a message that you need to be giving from the time your daughter is very young, and if you've been doing that, then it will make it easier to connect it to sex. (And if you have a son then you should be giving him the same message.) I believe that this message, especially combined with the message about disease, will have some effect. Blow jobs are easy to give. You don't even have to get undressed. Oral sex on a woman is a much more complicated process. You need more privacy. It takes more time. And guys don't have the peer pressure to perform oral sex on their girlfriends that girls do, and so they're less likely to push past any natural reticence that they have about licking a vagina. So with these messages, you'll be putting up a hurdle. It may be one that will only last a few months, but it could also push this particular act off for a year or two, so it's worth undergoing the added stress on you that this discussion will have.

STDs

Even though I've written 31 books, when I write a book that has a lot of information about sexually transmitted diseases, I always make sure that it is vetted by a medical doctor. There are so many of these diseases and the information about them changes so rapidly that it is very hard even for me to keep up. And if you're in a monogamous relationship, you had no reason to know more than some passing information about STDs until you had teenage children. But if you have teenagers, then it's time to become better informed. A lot better informed.

I know that scare tactics don't work. I already gave you the example of the films shown to soldiers in the two world wars. But while giving your teen all the gory details of the many sexually transmitted diseases won't stop him from having sex if he's ready, you can at least push your teen toward making sure that he always use condoms. Although condoms don't offer 100% protection, they do offer some, and they're certainly better than nothing. Teens in general have gotten this message, as condom use is up and unintended pregnancies among teens are down, so your job is to make sure that your teen gets this message. And to do that, you're going to have to study up.

However, this isn't the book where you're going to get those lessons. I'd need to devote an entire chapter to the subject because when protecting oneself against STDs a little information might be more dangerous than none. You'll either have to get another book or look up "sexually transmitted diseases" online. (The Centers for

Disease Control and Prevention or Planned Parenthood would be good places to start.) But I do want to pass on a few facts that I think need to be highlighted. The first is that STDs aren't like the common cold, where if you're exposed to the virus, either you're going to get the cold and know it, or you won't get it. Most people who are infected with an STD don't know it right away. That's because they get no visible symptoms or the symptoms won't show up for quite some time. But if they're infected, they can still pass the disease on, and the next person may exhibit a full-blown case right away. So asking potential partners whether they've ever had a disease doesn't offer much protection, because they could have a disease and not know it. The only way to know for sure is to be tested. Now is a 16-year old who's madly in love and has decided to have sex going to ask a partner to get tested? I doubt it. But knowing all the risks, will that teenager agree to limit those risks by insisting that a condom be used? Here I think the answer might well be yes. Just as you may not get a teenage driver to always obey the speed limits but can get them to always wear a seat belt, you may not get a teenager to remain abstinent but can get that teen to use condoms.

Another fact I want to highlight is about AIDS. Today some people have this idea that AIDS is not as serious as it once was because there are ways of extending the life of someone who gets infected. There are too many young gay men having unprotected sex these days, and with AIDS spreading quickly among heterosexuals, this is one myth that you must make sure your child doesn't believe. Again, fear may not stop someone from having sex, but it may at least make them more cautious.

And finally, since I did write a book about herpes, I offer a couple of random facts about that disease. The first is that genital herpes can be transmitted without any genitals coming into contact. The reason is that your partner could have a patch on his or her thigh or backside that is shedding viruses that obviously a condom couldn't protect against. I recently met a reporter from a college newspaper as part of my show on mtvU. She interviewed some of the students at her school, asking them about their thoughts on testing. Too many—for her taste, I might add—said that as long as the person looked "clean" they wouldn't worry about getting a disease from him or her. As you can see with regard to herpes, you don't have to have even one small blemish, and yet you could still pass on the disease. I understand that these students were talking about the person's overall appearance, but I'm saying that even a careful examination of a potential partner's every square inch wouldn't be enough to guarantee against the transmission of an STD. So getting your teenager to understand that looks can be very deceiving must be part of the message you communicate.

The other fact about herpes that needs to be reported is that having herpes makes you much more susceptible to AIDS. Almost every country that has had an AIDS epidemic had a herpes epidemic first. Having the herpes lesions makes you much more prone to be infected by HIV if you come into contact with the virus. So while herpes itself won't kill you, it could have more serious consequences.

Setting Standards

I want to return to something that I mentioned in Chapter 1—the fact that European teens are just as sexually active as Americans but have fewer unintended pregnancies and abortions. I can't tell you what morals to pass on to your children, so if you are dead set against giving even a hint that you would accept your teen to be sexually active, then that's the message that you have to give. But if you're wondering what message to give, and especially if you weren't married when you first had sex and so feel duplicitous asking your kids to be more virtuous than you were, I suggest that you adopt the European model. Obviously, I'm not telling you to offer your teen the keys to a motel room after he or she has been dating the same person for 6 months, but you can certainly give the message that casual sex is completely wrong but sex within a relationship, even if it is not marriage, may be right for some people.

How do you give that message? First, give your teen as much trust as is warranted. Each teen is different and reaches a different level of maturity at a different age, so I can't say to you that no 14-year-old should be having sex and every 18-year-old is ready, because neither is true in the absolute sense, even though it is true in general. But if you're constantly butting heads about his or her love life, then your opinion won't count for as much on the important issue of when to have sex. So, for example, if your first impression of the guy your daughter is dating is "Yuck," try to spend some time together to get to know him better. Try to see what she sees in him. Maybe you'll change your mind, but at least she'll get the message that you're trying. Remember, some teens aren't sure if they're ready for sex, but do it out of rebellion. So remove that as a motivator by showing a willingness to listen.

If you know any young couples who are clearly having sex—maybe a cousin who is living with her boyfriend but not married—let it be known that you approve, or at least are not against their lifestyle. At the same time, let your teen know how you feel about casual sex. Believe me, your message will get through.

And look around for other positive and negative messages. Sadly, these days there are far too many young celebrities living the high life and paying a severe price for it. Talk about it with your kids. Don't go overboard being negative, but instead stress how sad it is.

Sex Ed Classes

What about sex ed classes? There may be several problems with them. The biggest these days is that many of them are only teaching about abstinence, omitting any information about contraception, because federal funding has pushed them in that direction. Studies have shown that while abstinence-only classes may—and underline the word *may*—work in the short term, they do not work in the long run. And then you're faced with students who after a time become sexually active but haven't been taught about contraception. So bear in mind that just because your child may have taken a sex ed class in school does not mean that she's been taught about contraception. To my way of thinking this is a serious mistake, but there's nothing I can do about it, nor can you. Therefore, if you know that the sex ed program in your child's school teaches abstinence only, then you have a duty to give your child the information she needs to protect herself.

But even if your child's school does offer a fuller program, the quality of the education in some of these classes can still be hit or miss for several reasons. Most important, is the teacher experienced and comfortable with the material? If not, then I have doubts about how much the students will learn. How good is the textbook? At what age is the class given? If your child may already be sexually active, then that would be too late, obviously. And what if your child does not understand something; is he or she going to ask the teacher for clarification? Probably not, unless the teacher is quite good. And if some of the other students later pass on information that is wrong, who will your child listen to, schoolmates or the teacher?

Speaking of what takes place in school, I will point out that the best indicator of whether a teen is going to be sexually active at a young age or not isn't the sex education program offered by the school, but how well the teen is doing in school overall. Marian Wright Edelman said, "The best contraception is a meaningful future." Kids who do well in school are the ones who have sex the latest. By making sure that your teen is doing as well as she can in all her classes, you are also putting off the time when she will first become sexually active. Obviously, there are many reasons that you want your child to do well in school, but maybe this one fact will give you a little more incentive to keep closer tabs on your teen's schoolwork.

Because of all these issues, my advice is for you to assume the responsibility of making sure your child has all the accurate information he or she needs. If you look at your child's textbook and find it adequate, and speak with the teacher and decide that this teacher has the proper training, then you could leave this subject matter in the hands of the professionals. Just don't assume that the sex ed classes your child attends will do the job without doing your homework.

The Moral Message

Obviously, if you have particular religious or moral beliefs that you want to have included in your child's sex education, that is something that you will have to provide. Most public schools are prohibited from including moral messages with the information about sexual functioning, so that's one area that's entirely under your control if your child goes to a public school. If your child goes to a parochial school, then perhaps you can trust the school to give him the proper moral instruction, but studies have shown that such instruction isn't taken very seriously by teens. In fact, any type of religious instruction has been shown to have a minimal impact on the sexual behavior of teens. So as I've said earlier, it's how you behave that will give your children the best lessons in morals, much more effectively than anything any educator or religious leader can say, or even what you say. Your actions end up being a very effective message that gets reinforced every day of the year, hopefully in a positive way. On the other hand, if what you do sets a negative example, then don't be surprised if your offspring pick that up.

All this doesn't mean that you shouldn't speak to your children about moral values. Far from it. The only problem is that young people today have a habit of listening with one ear with an iPod plugged into the other, and they don't always get the full message you want them to hear. If you're trying to get them to pick up on a particular set of moral values, even if they go to a house of worship every week, take religious classes, and hear you speak ad nauseum about how evil the world is, they still may not quite get it. The responsibility of passing on a set of morals is in your hands, and to accomplish that you have to speak to your child directly and make sure your behavior sets the proper tone, because you must never forget that you are the most important role model in your child's life.

There's an organization, the National Campaign to Prevent Teen and Unplanned Pregnancy, that stresses the messages I've been giving in this chapter. On their Web site (www.teenpregnancy.org), they offer "10 Tips for Parents to Help Their Children Avoid Teen Pregnancy." These tips pretty much echo what I've been saying here. The bottom line is that it's your overall relationship with your child that counts. At the end of these tips they point out that it's never too late to get closer to your child. I'm of the opinion that it's never too late to try anything, so you should certainly never give up on your relationship with your children. But one also has to be realistic, and if a teenager—who is really a lot more adult than child—has chosen a particular path, it's very hard to make an impact. That's why it's so much better to begin as early as possible to set the right examples for your children, to watch closely what they are doing, and to exert as much authority as you can to lead them in the right direction.

Homosexuality

While we don't know for certain the etiology or source of homosexuality, there is sufficient evidence to believe that the genetic component is the strongest one. This means that for most gays and lesbians, their very first sexual feelings are for people of their own sex, and they can begin to sense this as early as 9 or 10 years old. What they will also sense is that being gay is not what their parents or society wants them to be. It should go without saying that you should love a gay child as much as a straight one, but that's not as easy as it sounds for some parents. The whole process of parenting a gay child is a complicated one (see Chapter 8 for more details).

Of course, with so much media coverage of homosexuality, it's possible now for parents or other family members to assume that a child is homosexual when that's not the case. Just because a girl shows characteristics of being a tomboy or a boy prefers to draw rather than play sports doesn't mean that she or he is gay. So don't overreact to your child's behavior. If your child's personality is different from what you expect, just be supportive and see what develops. Protect your child from being teased, to the degree that you can, and offer them as much room as you can to grow in the direction they're headed. Some will make a sudden switch back to the mainstream while others will continue to forge new paths, be it with regard to their sexuality or other traits. Society used to frown on people who were different, so much so that even being left-handed was a quality associated with the devil and was forcefully "corrected." Now we know better. We understand that our genes are complex and can create a myriad of different types of people. If you discover that your child is headed off on his own, encourage him as best you can. And as with sex, learn as much as you can about the direction toward which he's headed so that you can still offer guidance, even if you have no personal experience in this area. You never stop being a parent, and there's great pleasure to be found when you can be of assistance when a child of any age looks to you for parenting.

For Parents of Younger Children

Though this is a book about teens, I realize that some parents of future teens may be reading this book too. Since our younger children know so much more because of their exposure to the media, I felt it important to also give some advice in this book on how to talk to younger children.

To illustrate what I just said, let me give you a story told by a friend. She'd decided to have "the talk" on the early side, when her daughter was only 9. She took her to her favorite restaurant and struggled to get the words out. At some point the discussion turned to body piercing, and her 9-year-old revealed that she knew all about the various places on their body that people get pierced. Her mother was stunned.

This example shows that it's never too young to have the talk, though obviously the conversation will be different depending on the child and the age of the child. But with so much information, and misinformation, floating around out there, "the talk" becomes an important tool not just for imparting information, but for finding out what types of information have already filtered into your child's mind.

With really young children, you know that they are not sexually active, and so the process is much less stressful. The most important advice I can give you with regard to younger children is not to give too much information. You can't be sure why a child is asking a question. Your son or daughter may have seen something on TV or heard something said by a friend and ask you about it, but that doesn't mean they want to hear the entire birds and bees talk. So answer any questions simply, and then ask them if they're satisfied with that answer. If they are, you can stop at that point. If they have more questions, then you can continue the discussion. I would recommend that you buy an age-appropriate book ahead of time. Let's say that you have a 6-year-old who hasn't asked any questions about sex yet. You may not feel the need to bring the subject up, and that's OK, but what if tomorrow morning that child starts asking you questions? It's better to be able to say, "Wait a second dear, let me get this book I bought that we can read together." By reading the book together, you'll have a road map of how to handle this topic in front of you.

What if your child never asks you any questions? Does that mean you should just shelve this topic? I don't think so, because if you make it a part of your parent/child relationship to talk about sex, it will be easier on both of you when your child is old enough that the potential for having sex has arrived. Obviously, it's not going to be a part of your daily conversations, but if a few times a year you've talked about sex together from the time your child started school, or even before if the subject comes up naturally, then when the teenage years arrive, it won't be quite as hard. It will be part of a continuum rather than a topic that comes out of the blue.

Nudity

I am often asked how old children should be to make it necessary for parents to cover up when the kids are around. The broad answer is that there is no set age, because children brought up among nudists don't suffer any consequences from seeing their parents nude throughout their life. But since most people are not nudists, there will come a time when you as parents, rather than the child, will feel uncomfortable being nude around your children, and as soon as you feel that way, start covering up. That doesn't mean that you need to worry if the child sees you stepping out of the shower, but it does mean that on a hot day when you might not want to wear any clothes if there were no kids around, you'll put on some minimal cover-ups.

Don't be surprised if it's your child who suddenly demands privacy long before you expected it. If you have a 2-year-old—who is out of diapers, of course—who doesn't want you to see him or her naked, then you should respect that right. It may seem silly, but if the child feels uncomfortable, then respect such wishes. On the other hand, if you have a 6-year-old who insists on walking around the house naked all the time, you have the right to explain that it's not acceptable, if that's the way you feel. Privacy is a two-way street and a family can set any rules it deems proper. You don't need my advice, you just have to settle into a comfort zone that is appropriate for everyone living under your roof.

What you mustn't do, however, is make a big deal out of this subject. Many people grow up to have body image problems, and they can be serious. If someone is married and doesn't want to be seen naked by his or her spouse, that puts a damper on their sex life and, in turn, on their relationship. So you don't want to tell a child that being naked is a terrible thing. You may think of the sexual implications of nudity, but children won't. Instead, they'll feel that there's something wrong with his or her body and that's why you want them to cover up. In my opinion, if you have to err on one side or the other, it's better to err on the side of too much nudity rather than too little. The message to children that their body is beautiful and natural is much too important to let them think the opposite. So the less of a big deal you make of this subject, the better.

Inappropriate Touching

Another issue that I'm often asked about when it comes to toddlers is masturbation. Many little ones, both boys and girls, touch their genitals. Why do they do that? Because it's pleasurable. Even if they can't have an orgasm, it still feels good to them, and as I said at the very beginning of this book, even babies in the womb can become aroused. But while no one can see what's going on in the womb, clearly it's a different story if it's happening in your living room. The key to dealing with such situations is that word *privacy* again.

You wouldn't hesitate to tell your daughter not to pick her nose in front of everyone, but if one's nose needs to be cleaned out, it has to be done, but it's something that we do *in private*. All you have to do is to give that same story to your daughter about touching herself "down there." Tell her there's nothing wrong with it, but it's something she should only do in private. What, then, if she's always rushing off to find some privacy in order to touch herself? Of course that's not common, so most parents won't have to worry about that particular scenario, but some children do become hooked on generating these feelings of pleasure. Each case is going to be a little different, but generally I think the solution is going to be to give such a child a little extra attention. In other words, distract the child by reading a book together or playing with some toy, or at the very least, if you have your hands full doing something else, making sure that the child has a toy she likes to play with instead of her genitals. You don't want to make your daughter feel that anything to do with her genitals is bad, because that can have negative effects when she grows older, but you also don't want her to act inappropriately around the family. So don't ignore such activity, but don't make too much of it either. In most cases, such behavior eventually will change on its own. If it doesn't, or if it is extreme, consult your pediatrician.

And what about the youngsters who are always trying to touch their parents in inappropriate places, or else siblings or other children who are around? Again, your explanation as to why this is not done goes back to the issue of privacy, but in such cases you can be a little bit sterner. The child probably knows he or she is doing something that is not supposed to be done, so rather than being an issue of sex, it is one of obedience. I'm afraid that far too many parents today are too lax with their children, but that's a subject for another book altogether.

Language

Some parents make a point of using the appropriate medical terms for body parts, saying *penis* and *vagina*. I'm all for that, but I'm also not against using other, less formal words. It really boils down to what you're comfortable with. You have to make sure your children understand what penis and vagina means, but since these are words that are hard for little children to pronounce, most parents begin using a simpler term when they're very young, like wee wee, and then that term sticks. I don't believe that's anything that you have to worry about. It's more important that 2-year-olds learn how to be toilet trained than use Latin terms for their body parts. So if changing the terminology is going to get them confused, it's better to stick with the childish terms that they understand and can pronounce. On the other hand, if a toddler totally mispronounces vagina but you understand her, that's fine too.

However, if you are embarrassed to say the words penis or vagina, and that's why you avoid using those terms in front of your children, then that's another story. As I've been saying, it's part of your responsibility as a parent to make sure that your child understands about sex. How are you going to have a serious conversation with your children as they grow up if you can't say penis and vagina comfortably? So if you're the one with the problem, then I would change my advice and tell you to begin using the correct terminology as soon as your child can master such words so that you get used to it and are ready for later conversations. And because you are going to have to have these conversations and it will seem silly to be speaking to a 16-year-old about his wee wee, then at some point you'd better teach your child the correct terminology and have both of you used to saying those words. But just as toddlers use many babyisms and eventually pick up the correct language, the same is true for the words for their genitals.

Interfering Relatives

While you may assume that you as parents are the ones who exercise most of the control over your children, the fact is that there are others who also have an influence, and most of those are related to your children.

How often do you hear a grandparent or an aunt or uncle asking a child, in a rather broad age range that can stretch from as young as 5 to certainly teens, whether or not they have a girlfriend or boyfriend? They think it's cute, but it ends up putting pressure on the child. If a 12-year-old gets the message from several close relatives that he or she is expected to have a girlfriend or boyfriend, that child is going to be affected by that message, especially if the relative pushes the conversation forward. As I've said several times in this book already, your child's privacy is important; so if you see a relative pressuring your child about his or her love life, you should step in and nip that conversation in the bud. It's not cute and it could have negative consequences.

Siblings

Of course there may be another set of relatives that lives in even closer proximity to a child—siblings. Older siblings could pass on information that is either inappropriate or wrong to a younger child. I understand that you can't watch your children every minute of the day, and I don't think that you need to assume that this will happen and say something in advance. What you must do is watch for behavioral changes. If a younger child's behavior changes, ask him or her what is going on, and if you can't get an answer, then take a closer look at how your kids are interacting. If you suspect that an older child is scaring a younger one with "facts," then you have to step in and take action. Siblings often tease each other, and it's usually harmless; but when it comes to sex, the consequences could be more serious, so it's something to be attuned to, but not overly so if there's no evidence of anything wrong.

Friends

When the children of my coauthor, Pierre Lehu, were younger, the father of one of their friends came to him to discuss something "serious": His daughter, then about 6 or 7, had seen a book about sex in Pierre's basement and had been asking questions. He was worried that it was an adult book. It turned out that the book was an age-appropriate book about sex that Pierre had given his children and the crisis was averted, but certainly lots of information about sex is passed between friends, and sometimes older kids like to show off by telling younger kids what they know about sex, information which may or may not have any truth to it at all.

It's because of this possibility that you have to make sure that your kids are given information about sex that comes from you, either orally or in the form of a book. Here again, I think the book offers more in the way of protection. If a 4-year-old heard something that he didn't understand, he'd probably come to you, but if a 10-year-old were put in that situation, he might be too embarrassed, especially if it involved ratting on a friend. But if there was a book in your house that your child had access to, he could get the needed, correct information without having to ask you. I'm not saying that your child shouldn't ask you—as I said you want to be an askable parent—but sex is one topic that we know causes embarrassment (imagine yourself talking to your doctor about a sexual problem), so you want there to be another avenue available to your child for the correct information to come through.

Sometimes young children also play "doctor" or some variation of that; in other words, they take off their clothes in front of each other. (This could just as easily occur with relatives such as cousins as with friends.) It's fairly common and really isn't a big deal, though obviously it's not something that you want to allow to continue once you discover it. Again, the explanation is that our bodies are private, and that's really all that needs to be said, unless one of the children involved is much older. Then this innocent playing could have more serious consequences. If that turns out to be the case, the older child cannot be left alone with the younger ones. Hopefully that will take care of it, but you must also talk to the younger children to make certain that no psychological damage has been done. Don't overreact, as you don't want to scare the child, but instead want to make sure that no ideas have been planted that might be troublesome to the child.

Protecting Children from Sexual Predators

There's nothing scarier than the thought of having your child stolen by someone intent on having sex with the child. On the other hand, you can't live your life in fear. Most children who are kidnapped are taken by one of their parents, not by a stranger; so while the danger exists, there isn't a predator lurking behind every tree. Nevertheless, you have to teach your children that the danger exists and what to do in case they encounter someone who wants to do them harm. The trick is getting them to pay attention without scaring them.

While I am normally not a fan of absolutes, in this case there's no room for ambiguity, which why teaching children *never* to talk to a stranger is a good idea. You don't have to explain to them why they shouldn't go with strangers, because it's far better if they err on the side of caution, maybe insulting a neighbor who is absolutely harmless, than making the wrong decision about a predator. By drumming into their heads that under no circumstances should they have any contact with strangers, you can at least be sure that they've understood you. Were you to give them any wiggle room, then they'd be more likely to make the wrong decision at the worst possible moment.

I would also say that you should get together with some of the other parents in the neighborhood and coordinate your activities with regard to keeping your children safe. If every child has received the same message, then the odds of everyone obeying will be stronger. In fact, the kids will be impressed if in addition to hearing this message from their parents, they also hear it from other parents, and impressing upon them the importance of this rule is what you want to do.

And while you're talking to other parents and neighbors, you should put together a system where everybody watches out for the kids in the neighborhood. At the most basic level, there should be a list of phone numbers—home, office, and cell—for every parent that is distributed to everyone on the block. That way even a neighbor who doesn't want to get involved can reach you. It would probably be a good idea for that list to include a photo of each child, so that neighbors who don't know the kids that well, and certainly not by name, could easily identify a child. Obviously, this is not a list that you want circulating widely, so if you do prepare a list like this, make sure that you know who is getting it. In other words, don't print out 50 copies, but only one copy for each person who should get it. If a neighbor says, "Can I have one for the man who lives next door?" gently say, "No," and that you'll contact him directly to see if he wants to participate. That way you and the other parents can keep control of who has the list and who doesn't.

One of the parents should be in charge of making sure that no sexual predators live in the area. I'm not sure how I feel about published lists of predators, but since they exist, you might as well use them. Just don't make yourself paranoid, because while it is very important to protect your children, it is also important to allow them to take risks. You can't protect them from every danger, and you don't want them to grow up afraid of their shadow. While I was worried when my daughter went off to join the Israeli army, I was also quite proud. You want to raise children who are not afraid to take risks; and so while you have to prepare them for the dangers they may face, be they predators or sexually transmitted diseases or unintended pregnancies or drunk drivers, you don't want to make your warnings so overpowering that they become afraid to do anything on their own.

For Boys

Most children don't know about homosexuality. Yes, there are some children raised by two men or two women, but for the vast majority, a child's parents consists of a man and a woman. When explaining to a daughter about the dangers of sexual predators, it will make sense to her to be wary of men. But that same advice may seem strange to a young boy. So you're going to have to do some explaining to a male child of the attraction that he offers. Being clueless isn't going to be of any help to him. But if he understands the nature of the danger, without necessarily knowing the details, then he'll have an easier time recognizing when he's in danger, and so be better able to protect himself.

At the same time, it's important to remember that most homosexuals are not pedophiles. Just because you are protecting your child doesn't mean that you want to make him homophobic. Clearly, there are heterosexual pedophiles as well as homosexual ones, so don't go out of your way to criticize homosexuals when giving your son an explanation of what to look out for.

And, of course, there are female sexual predators, though there are far fewer of them. But you mustn't let your children think that a stranger is safe just because she's a woman, for not only are there sexual predators who are women, but there are also other women used by sexual predators to lure in young children.

For Girls

Eating disorders are not my specialty nor part of the focus of this book, but because they are of epidemic proportions among teenage girls, I do want to say a few words about anorexia and bulimia. There are many reasons that young girls develop eating disorders, but certainly there is a sexual connotation to wanting to be thin, since in our society being thin is a component of being sexually attractive. If a girl has low self-esteem, then whatever her weight, she could begin to focus on it and develop an eating disorder. Parents who place too much emphasis on their daughters' appearance, because they want them to be sexy so as to be able to attract the right man, may be doing terrible damage. So rather than making too big a deal about a daughter's appearance, I would suggest that parents concentrate on building up their daughters for whatever positive qualities they have rather than emphasizing their physical aspects. The phenomenon of giving 16-year-olds breast implants as a sweet-sixteen present clearly passes on the wrong message to these girls. Just keep in mind that if you place too much importance on the way your daughter looks, one result might be that she ends up developing an eating disorder.

CHAPTER 4

Counteracting
Peer Pressure

PEER PRESSURE IS a reality that you can't ignore. No matter how close your child feels to you, as kids get older, they must separate; and to gain the strength they need to help them break away, they cling together in groups of their peers, and those peers have a tremendous amount of influence. And ever since modern media arrived on the scene, that influence has become even stronger because now the group of peers influencing your teen is no longer limited to those in your neighborhood or your child's school but has been broadened to include a vast ocean of teens across the country and even around the world, as well as the adults who market to them. The country you live in will affect the peer pressure on your teen, as we've seen when it comes to the different attitudes among teens in different parts of the world with regard to premarital sex.

Are you necessarily alone in fighting this peer pressure? Of course not. First of all, it takes two parents to make a child, so unless the other parent of your child is out of the picture entirely, you should have an ally, though it's vital that you work together. I'll have more to say on parenting as a team in a bit. You also have a family, and your family members can play an important role in bringing up your children. How close your teen is to grandparents, aunts and uncles, cousins, and so on is going to be different within each family, but if you know how to make use of these family members, then they can prove to be very good allies. Then there are the groups you belong to, including the teen's teachers, your neighbors, your place of worship, and any organizations to which you may belong. The more that negative peer pressure is having an effect on your teen, the more you may need to use these resources.

As I've mentioned in Chapter 1, the value system being propagated in the United States is quite different from that in many European countries. Here, many parents are pressing the message that teens should abstain from having sex until they are married. There are major campaigns pushing abstinence in our houses of worship and in our schools. In Europe, on the other hand, abstinence is not the primary message. The basic message that European teens are getting is to have only responsible sex, which is to say sex within a relationship and using contraception. And this message isn't fed to European teens only via their parents and schools, but also through peer pressure. So while teens on both sides of the Atlantic are having sex at about the same rate, the rate of unintended pregnancies and abortion are higher in the United States than in Europe.

When you send your teen a message that is the total opposite of the message that your teen is getting from his or her peers, you're setting a trap for your teen. Let's take the message about abstinence. When you set the bar very high, once a teen decides that he or she can't live within that boundary, that teen is set adrift. Once a teen has breached the boundaries set by his parents—in this case by having sex, which may be limited to oral sex (which is still a banned activity from the parents' point of view)—he is now outside the influence of parental guidelines altogether. If his parents have been adamant about not engaging in any sexual activity and he's gone ahead and had sex in one form or another, then as far as he's concerned he's lost his parents' blessings and he may as well continue to engage in this sexual activity, and others. But because European teens have been permitted to have sex if they're in a serious relationship, those who are having sex that is within a relationship and includes the use of birth control are within the scope of their parent's guidance. They can retain their parent's approbation and still have sex as long as they stick to the rules their parents have set. And so that's what they are doing, which in turn has meant that they are having fewer unintended pregnancies and fewer abortions. And the more that European teens are acting responsibly, according to European society at least, the more peer pressure there is among those teens to act responsibly too, adding to the overall strength of the message.

Let me be very clear on this point because it's an important one. If you lay down very strict limits on your children but they're limits that they are not likely to obey, once they've disobeyed you, you've lost most, if not all, of your influence over them with regard to that topic. Let me give you an example from another sphere, the drinking of alcohol. Some parents say to their teens, "If you're not in shape to come home because you've had too much to drink, call me and I'll come get you, no questions asked." The teens of those parents are much more likely to get home safely than teens whose parents say, "If I find you've been drinking alcohol, I'm going to kill you." Those teens, if they find themselves drunk, wouldn't dare ask for help, and so must get home on their own, which might mean driving home while drunk or accepting a ride from someone who has been drinking.

I understand the conflict faced by parents. You want to be the opposing force to peer pressure. You want to lay down the law, knowing full well that your teen is not going to obey you 100% of the time, just as you did not obey your parents. And as I said earlier, you can't be "friends" with your teen because you do want your teen to look at you as an authority figure. And yet, you have to find a compromise position because if you are too tough, that's not going to work either. If you put too much pressure on your teen, if your teen feels too conflicted between the rules you are laying down and what his or her peers are saying to do, the result will likely be that at some point your teen is going to give in to peer pressure and break the strict rules you've put down. If you put your teenager between that rock and a hard place, either your teen will rebel, and then you've lost all control, or your teen will crack under the pressure, enduring psychological damage.

The very fact that one is a teenager means that one is supposed to be learning how to operate on one's own, that one is well on the way to becoming an adult. If a teen is put in a position where he is completely suffocated by rules, then he won't be able to grow up as he should. So something will have to give, which will either be your rules or his ability to turn into a man.

I realize that some of you reading this are going to disagree with me. You're going to say, "I'm a tough parent and what I say goes, period. If I tell my son he has to be home by 12, he better be or he's grounded. And if I say no sex, I mean no sex. He may not like it now, but in the long run he'll thank me." I'm not saying such an attitude can never work, but these days, for most parents, it's a lot harder to pull off. In most homes in the twenty-first century, both parents work and they often work long hours. So if you're not around to keep track of what your teen is doing, how can you enforce your rules? You may be able to enforce some of them, but if your teen feels under tremendous pressure because of that, he's likely to find other ways of breaking the rules, like having sex with his girlfriend at 4 in the afternoon when no one is home, or smoking pot or using the family computer for some sort of illegal downloading. A teenager is really an adult and if you try to make your daughter feel like a child, she's going to rebel. Maybe she'll cut her nose to spite her face and not get the straight A's she's capable of. Or she'll post pictures of her bare breasts on some Web page. The fact is, if a teen is stewing in her own anger for hours on end, it's going to cause problems of one sort or another. You can't turn your home into a jail, so being overly strict will probably backfire. Maybe not in every case, but I guarantee you it won't work most of the time.

Of course, every individual is different so each set of parents and teens have to work out their own way of navigating this growing-up process. So many changes have taken place over the last generation or two that many of the guidelines that kept those choices in a narrow range have disappeared. So if you think it's more difficult raising a teen today, you're absolutely correct. You can't absolutely follow the same set of guidelines your parents laid down for you because the situation has changed so much, especially in the area of technology, and the changes keep right on coming. I'm going to deal with those changes in greater detail in other chapters, but here I need to acknowledge that those changes have also affected peer pressure. For example, if a teen feels forced to have a page on MySpace or Facebook where he or she has to reveal so much about his or her life, suddenly the closed doors of the family's bosom, which for so long offered a safe haven, are thrown wide open. We don't know the long-term ramifications of this, so how can we be sure of what needs to be done to adapt to this new phenomena?

How to Counter Peer Pressure Successfully

As the dangers multiply, it's only natural that parents will want to protect their children, but smothering them is not going to work, either in the short run or the long run. What you have to do is help them grow up, which means you have to give them more responsibility, not less. If you can no longer just lay down laws that will stop peer pressure in its tracks, then you have to make sure that your teens are prepared to handle this pressure on their own.

How do you manage this? With a plan, persistence, patience, and teamwork.

The Plan

It is vital that parents work together to raise their children. When they take opposite sides, the children quickly learn how to manipulate these divisions, and by playing one parent off of the other, they get their way. So if the two of you are going to set a curfew, decide together what it is going to be, and don't vary it without checking with each other. Certainly, there can be reasons to vary a curfew, but if you consistently counterman each other's orders, then it becomes a game that your teen will be playing, and probably winning.

Q. My wife and I have disagreed about how to raise our son since he was a little boy. She didn't want him to play with guns, and I thought he should be allowed to play with them. If he got into a fight, she'd yell at him; I'd teach him how to get the other guy the next time. I wanted him to take judo lessons; she refused. You get the picture. I want him to be a man's man, and if she had her way, he'd turn out to be a sissy. When it comes to sex, I know the dangers and I want him to be safe, but I also want him to know how to have a good time. My wife, on the other hand, is going to give him so many warnings about how dangerous sex can be that I'm afraid he's going to remain a virgin forever. He's eleven, and seems like a normal kid, despite his mother's always trying to protect him. No matter what my

wife says, I intend to take him camping one day soon and tell
him the truth about sex. I'm right to want him to be a man's man,
especially when it comes to sex, right?

A. From what I can gather, the end result of this man-to-man
talk is that you're going to be pressuring him to have sex sooner
rather than later, and more important, perhaps sooner than he's
going to be ready. If you're lucky it will be with someone he cares
for, and if not, it could be with some girl who's slept with dozens of
guys and will give him a sexually transmitted disease.

When he was younger, your disagreements with your wife
weren't as consequential. But if he gets the message from you that
it's OK to disobey Mom, then he could start making mistakes that
will be life-threatening, such as drinking and driving, taking drugs,
and having sex with the wrong people. I understand that you don't
want him to be tied to his mother's apron strings, but the best way
to accomplish that is to talk with your wife and come to a consen-
sus on the messages that you're going to give him. You may both
have to make some compromises, but in the long run, by having a
unified parenting front, your son will be better off.

Curfews

With regard to curfews, and possibly other rules as well, I would
encourage you to talk to the parents of your teen's friends. It doesn't
matter if all the teens in a group have the same curfew, but if several do, then it's easier for that subgroup to leave whatever activity is going on together. If your teen has the earliest curfew, that's
a very difficult situation for him to handle and will create added
conflict. And since I'm a believer in white lies, I say you don't have
to tell your teen about such conversations (though for that to be
effective, all the parents involved have to keep mum about these
secret negotiations.) While it might seem underhanded, you're actually doing your teen a favor. Your teen might not want to stay out
till all hours, she may prefer to get home at a reasonable hour so
that she won't be too sleepy in class, but because of peer pressure,
she'll have a hard time going home on her own. But if she is part of
a group that has to be home at, say midnight, then it makes it that
much easier on everybody.

Positive Reinforcement

But your game plan cannot be all negative and only place limits. There also have to be rewards. If your child gets good grades, for example, then she has to be given more trust when setting the rules. Curfews are something where there is a lot of peer pressure and so I believe they are important for the parents to set; but when it comes to other uses of private time, if your teen is discharging her responsibilities with regard to schoolwork and household chores, then it's unfair to tell her not to spend so much time chatting on the computer with her friends. Teens are learning many things while they're under your care, including how to be social, and so you have to understand the legitimacy of their social networks.

I have to admit that I'm giving you this advice after I took what I now believe was the wrong stance when my daughter was a teen. She wanted her own phone, but I didn't want to give it to her, so we fought constantly about how much time she spent on our phone line because we needed it too. I know now that I should have given her that phone line to avoid this set of conflicts. She'd earned the right by doing well in school, and I failed to recognize the importance of her being in communication with her friends at night, even though they did spend all day together in school. Just because when I was her age something like a private phone for a teen would have been an unheard-of luxury didn't mean it was that much of a luxury item in the years she was growing up.

Therefore, in drawing up your plan, put down what goals your teen has to meet and the rewards for meeting them. If your teen doesn't live up to her side of the bargain, then together you'll have to take appropriate action. But if the goals are set at the appropriate level—remember, not every student is going to get straight As—then I bet that most teens will happily accept the responsibilities in return for being treated more like adults.

Family as Team

While I encourage your teen to be given as much responsibility as he can handle, I think one way of helping him is to make your family a bit into a team. It may be obvious that cutting the grass or doing a load of wash is done for the family as whole, but so should getting good grades or earning a salary by mom or dad. By making the family into a team, you're actually causing another type of peer pressure, which will counterbalance to some degree the outside peer pressure. Sure it's good to get an A for oneself, but if it's also for the family as a whole, that will add some more impetus. And if everyone in the family is involved, your teen won't think that he's the only one being picked on. (Assuming you have more than one child, and also assuming they're not of equal abilities, make sure that you set goals that can be met, maybe setting a higher goal for one in academics and for another in sports or volunteering.)

Having made this suggestion, I want to caution you not to go overboard, like having team shirts made with the family crest or keeping constant score on a blackboard. This message needs to be given, but in a subtle way. And it's not just about getting ahead, it's also about moral values, helping others both in the family and outside, doing the best job even at mundane chores, caring about the planet, and so on. If these positive messages are given in small but regular doses, they will definitely have a positive effect. The point is to get them to look beyond themselves and their small group of friends and see that they have a place in the world, that their lives have more meaning than just hanging out with their friends, and that some of it starts with their family.

The Wrong Kind of Friends

Every parents' nightmare is that their child starts hanging out with the wrong type of friends—those who don't care about schoolwork, who drink and use drugs, who are sexually promiscuous, who seem to have no purpose in life or maybe are even into criminal activity. If your teen is in such a group, it may not be entirely his "fault." For whatever reason, this group may be the only one that is open to him. Your son could be faced with the choice of either being with this set of friends or having no friends at all. If that's the case, no matter what you say, your son is not going to abandon this set of peers.

What can you do if caught in this bind? No matter what you do, it's going to be difficult. I recommend adopting the underlying principle of martial arts in your parenting: In jujitsu and the like, the idea is to turn the opponent's power against them. (Though I was trained to be a sniper as an Israeli freedom fighter, I am not an expert in these arts, so please don't get upset if I'm not getting my facts about martial arts exactly straight as they're for illustrative purposes only.) Your teen wants desperately to be with his friends, so rather than telling him that he can't, tell him exactly what he has to do in order to be with them. In other words, if he keeps his grades up and does his chores diligently, then you're not going to harp on who his friends are. If he doesn't, then he can't see them.

The major effect of this method is that you are not constantly saying bad things about his friends. Why is that important? Because you're not going to be able to convince him of their weaknesses, no matter what you say. Since the odds are that you won't be able to keep him away from them all the time, in the long run he's going to disobey you and see them anyway; and as a result, you will have less and less influence on his life because the more he disobeys you, the easier it becomes. You will fight over it, but because his desire to be with his friends will be stronger than your desire to keep them out of his life, little by little he'll wear you down and as you stop enforcing what you say, he'll have less and less regard for what you say.

Moreover, if you keep putting his friends down, what you're doing is making a value judgment. In matters of taste, it is really hard to prove your case because people are entitled to their own opinions. Your teen is going to say to himself, "My parents like 1970s music, so what do they know about my tastes and my friends?" So what you have to do is not make it about this set of friends, but keep the focus on your son's actions, because those are under your control to some degree. If he's spending too much time with a bunch of losers, then he's not going to be able to get the grades he should, and so he'll be grounded until he does. He may get angry and blame you, but the disagreement will only be about his actions—the grades on his report card—not those of people over whom you have no control.

A program like this is going to be very demanding of you. If you think your daughter might be drinking, then you're going to have to tell her that she has to come talk to you when she comes home, not just slink off to her room, so you can decide whether or not she's sober. If she doesn't, she's grounded. If she does and you can smell alcohol on her breath, she's grounded. What will probably happen, assuming that her friends are drinking, (which is why you set up these rules in the first place) is that she'll limit her drinking so she can at least fake sobriety and suck a lot of mints before going home so you hopefully won't smell the alcohol on her breath (though a very minty breath should also be a dead give-away), not because she wants to obey you more than give in to the peer pressure of her friends, but because she'll want to continue to be able to see them. That's what I mean about using the power of her friends to your advantage. You'll be using her desire to be with this set of friends to get her to drink less. I would assume if this set of friends drinks that she'll have to drink a little to be a part of this group, and since having one beer isn't going to do much damage, I would advise not making a big deal about it. I'm not saying to tell her it's okay to drink, only that if you believe she's limiting her drinking, then you don't have to come down as hard on her.

Of course the best plan of action would be to get your son or daughter to hang out with a different set of kids. Is there anything that you can do that is proactive with regard to your teen's friends? It may not be easy, I can give you a few suggestions:

- Send your teen to summer camp, making sure it's one where the teens you don't want to be associated with your child aren't going. Let's say your son liked basketball and did play with one group of teens, but socially he hung out with another group that you didn't like. If you sent him to basketball camp for the summer, hopefully along with some of his basketball-playing friends, the bonding that went on during the summer might take hold during the next school year. It's not something that you can force to happen, but it's better than not doing anything. And if he got good enough, maybe he'd make the team, and then he'd definitely have a new set of friends. At the very least, he will have spent the weeks at camp away from his set of loser friends. Perhaps seeing what more desirable kids are like for a long period will get your child to see his old friends in a new light and start to spend less time with them.
- If your daughter is not getting the grades you believe she should be getting and you blame it on the group of friends

she has, hire someone from her class whom you would like her to be friends with to act as a tutor. You can't tell a teen to be friends with someone you choose for them; it never works. But if you can find an excuse to put two teens together over a period of time, such as having one tutor the other, a friendship might develop. If nothing else, her grades may start to improve.

- If your house of worship is involved in a charitable activity like a soup kitchen, insist that your son take part. Don't say it's because you want him hanging out with the other teens who are doing this voluntarily, but say that if he wants money to go out, he has to earn it this way. Again, the hope is that eventually he may like some of these teens and spend some time with them away from the soup kitchen.

As I said earlier, your daughter may know deep down inside that her friends are losers, but for some reason she hasn't been able to join another set of friends. Kids can be cruel, and it may not really be her fault that she has no choice but to associate with these kids, who also may not be totally at fault. While she won't admit it, she may want a different set of friends, but she doesn't know how to go about getting them, and she is going to be fiercely loyal to her old friends because they are her social lifesaver. So you have to find creative and canny ways to help her out of this situation. Rather then butt heads with her, try to think outside the box, finding different means to get her to meet other people. Once she makes these new connections, the odds are that she'll divide her social life, if not abandon her initial group of friends, of her own volition.

Controlling Sexual Behavior

Of all the banned activities a teen might be doing, sex is the hardest to control. There may be no physical evidence that you can point to in proving whether or not your son or daughter has just had sex. Sex doesn't take a lot of time, and your teen could be having sex at 3:30 in the afternoon, when you're both at work, and there'd be no way of telling. Or would there?

Some kids are very good at sneaking around and could keep their sex life quiet, but I believe that most kids will give themselves away, in one way or another. Maybe they'll use the bed and forget to make it, or leave a used condom in the garbage where it can be found. In other words, if you suspect inappropriate activity and you remain vigilant, I think that you will discover the truth. Of course if you do decide to play detective and learn that your child is having sex, what you then do about it is another story. No matter how angry you get, no matter what the punishment, I think the teen is going to find a way to have sex, particularly if it's not casual sex but at least one of the two teens involved has a crush on the other. So rather than look at the evidence you find as the means to punish your son or daughter, look at it as a cry for help. Don't make an all out effort to stop your teen from having sex (unless you can discover that it's casual sex) but instead make a concerted effort to make sure that your teen's sex life doesn't result in an unintended pregnancy or sexually transmitted disease. And rather than giving up, tighten up with regard to your teen's responsibilities. It's not about making him pay a price for being sexually active, but rather forcing as much responsibility as possible on him so that he understands that if he's going to act like an adult by having sex, then he's going to be treated as one in every other way.

There's no one formula to employ when thrusting responsibility on your teen. If your teen is capable of getting all As but hasn't been getting top marks, then demand that she start improving her grades and don't put too much added stress on her by heaping tons of household chores onto her schedule. On the other hand, if she's not going to be an A student, then insist she shine in other ways, such as by going to help at a local soup kitchen or volunteer at a nursing home. And if she does, praise her for it. It's not a punishment for having sex so much as a means of making her understand what it means to be responsible.

An Infinite Memory

In talking to your teens about peer pressure, there's another discussion that I urge you to have. While they may be breaking your rules in ways that are different from how you broke your parents' rules, there has been another significant change since you were a teen. If you got caught doing something that you shouldn't have been doing, unless it was criminal and you were arrested, after a time you could repair your reputation. In fact, the news about most of what you did, good or bad, was contained within a small community. Today that is no longer true. With every teen having a page on MySpace, Facebook, or some other social networking or social utility site (even *Playboy* is getting into the act), your teen's activities, whether he reports them himself or his friends do, are being pasted into the Internet in perpetuity. (I'll have more to say about social networking sites in another chapter, but this particular point needs to be made here because it forces a change on how teens react to peer pressure.)

Recently Miss New Jersey almost lost her title because of pictures that she posted on MySpace. These photos contained no nudity, but were a little suggestive, and mostly plain silly. Luckily for her, the state officials allowed her to retain her crown, but the reason the photos were brought to public attention in the first place was that someone tried to blackmail her with them, and she wisely showed them to the officials herself to blunt this attempted blackmail. This type of situation is going to occur more and more often. And while she had placed these photos on the Internet herself, a friend could have done it just as easily.

There are no limits when it comes to the extent or life of information that can now be shared. High school pranks can now haunt a person, not just for years, but forever. When companies are looking to hire someone, and there are dozens of applicants from which to choose, you can be sure they're going to drop the ones on whom a cursory Web search turns up anything negative. Is it worth giving up a dream job because peer pressure led you into cheating on a test or pulling some prank?

As a parent, you obviously know the answer to that, but the question is, how do you get that message through to a teen? First, make sure that this message isn't just conveyed to your teen but to everyone at his school. Either through the PTA, or on your own, find some expert who can talk about this subject and get the school to have a presentation to the whole school about it. And part of that presentation should be actual cases, like that of Miss New Jersey, so that the students can see concrete examples of what can happen, not just hear about the potentiality. Not everyone in that audience will thoroughly get the message, but enough will that it will add a dose of peer pressure on the side of being more cautious. This is similar to the effective campaign against drinking and driving. Most teens do make sure that there is one person who remains sober because it's been drummed into them that there always has to be a designated driver, so similar messages can also get through by addressing teens as a group rather than just individually.

(Though this is not exactly within the scope of this book, I feel I must point out a new danger regarding driving, cell phones. Even more dangerous than talking on them while driving is texting, because then you have to be looking at the tiny screen rather than the road. If you're not aware of this danger, please be forewarned, and lay down the law. Let your teen know that text messages appear on your bill and if you see any that took place while your teen was driving, both cell phone and car privileges will be taken away.)

Second, be vigilant at finding other examples in the media or online that will back up this point, then make sure that your teen reads them. Your teen may roll her eyes each time you tell her, "Read this," but that doesn't mean the message won't get through, at least eventually.

As I said, fear only goes so far in preventing people from making mistakes, but there's another emotion you can use: guilt. Remind your teen that if he gets caught doing something that will embarrass him, it is also going to embarrass every member of the family, and that embarrassment won't last for a day or two or be contained, but because of the Internet, these days the news will be spread far and wide and live online in perpetuity. If you've been trying to build up the family-as-a-team spirit I spoke about, then this argument should also exert some pressure on your teen.

There is a reverse side to this: Your teen is probably going to be watching over your shoulder to make sure that her parents are also towing the line. You may get annoyed when she points out that you're going over the speed limit or watering the lawn during a dry spell or not recycling that piece of aluminum foil, but rather than get annoyed, be thankful. She may be spying on your behavior in part to get back at you for making her toe the line, but it means she's also watching her own actions. That doesn't mean she'll never make a mistake, including ones induced by peer pressure, but hopefully it will happen less often and on less severe matters.

And something else you can do is to use these new methods of communicating to boast whenever your teen does something that deserves praise. It can be an e-mail blast or a family page on one of these social sites, but let friends and family know when your teen has received good grades or made the team. Your teen is going to be embarrassed, maybe even beg you not to do it, but deep down he will feel proud. And the more you build him up, the harder it will be for him to risk his reputation. If you show that you value it as much as possible, he can't help but to add value to it himself.

Admit Your Mistakes

One of the revelations that teenagers experience at some point is that their parents aren't perfect. Younger children believe that their mom and dad are just the greatest at everything, but since none of us adults is actually perfect, our faults eventually become evident to our teens. That can be a rude awakening, as well as an excuse that they may use to justify their own imperfect actions.

At the same time, many teens also think that they are superior to their parents, which they are in areas that matter to them most, like being hip to the latest trends. To some degree they need to feel this way in order to cut the apron strings. Where problems sometimes arise is when a child feels that he cannot live up to the standards of his parents, and rather than try, he just gives up.

One way of synthesizing these differing views your teens have of you, as a way to help them combat peer pressure, is to admit to your mistakes. I'm not telling you to confess every fault you might have. Remember I am a big advocate of privacy, so please keep your teenage indiscretions to yourself. No, what I'm talking about are mistakes you make in the present. Let's say you were checking out at the supermarket with your teen and you're in a rush and the cashier makes some mistake and you bark at her. At the time, your emotions got the better of you, but a few minutes later, in the car, you realize that you were wrong. Don't keep that news to yourself, but say it out loud so that your teen hears you say you were wrong.

Why is this important? First of all, your teen was listening to you and while he may not have said anything, he was thinking, "What's with Mom? Why is she being so ridiculous?" So if you later admit you were wrong, he'll have a better understanding of the situation and of you. Where you'd sunk a point or two in his view, you'll actually go up a few notches for admitting you were wrong.

But it will also be sending the message that it's OK for him to admit that he can be wrong, not only to you, but also to himself. I'm sure you've seen a movie or cartoon where an individual has a little angel on one shoulder and a devil on the other, each trying to push him in a certain direction. Peer pressure often assumes the role of that little devil. Now we all listen to that little devil from time to time, but just because we went off in the wrong direction for a few steps doesn't mean that we have to continue down that path forever. If we can admit that we're making a mistake, we can reverse course. So learning to admit mistakes is a very important quality. And your children learn many of their operating skills from you and how you live your life, and if you never admit to making a mistake, they also will have a hard time doing it.

Admitting mistakes, then, is a sort of safety valve that allows us to make a mistake and then correct it. While there are some positive aspects to peer pressure (such as when every one of your teen's friends intends to go to college, which makes him want to try as hard as possible too), we also know that peer pressure is pushing our teens off the straight and narrow path. But in order to make sure they're equipped with the skill set of how to reverse course when they obey negative peer pressure, we have to set the proper example in the first place.

Forgetting peer pressure for a moment, the very fact of being a teenager is a state in which you have to make mistakes. You can't listen blindly to everything you're told and be an adult. You have to learn how to make decisions, and the fact is that not every decision you're going to make is going to be correct, since none of us is perfect. Even though we adults are prone to make mistakes too, we should be making fewer of them because we have more experience. But a teen who is building up his core of experiences is necessarily also building up his share of mistakes and therefore needs to learn how to deal with those mistakes as quickly as possible.

That's why the example you set with regard to mistakes is so important. Don't try to protect your reputation as Mr. or Ms. Perfect Parent, but instead demonstrate to your teen that you know how to handle mistakes so that he'll learn that same skill set from you.

> Q. My husband is still friends with many of his high school buddies. Every year they all get together for a picnic in our backyard and after they've had a few beers, they start reminiscing about some of their exploits, many of which involved getting drunk. My 15-year-old son has heard these stories a thousand times, and the other day when I was trying to warn him about the dangers of drinking, he brought up his dad's example, saying he turned out all right. How do I handle that?

A. Of course your husband and his friends should have been aware of the potential damage their bragging might have, but it's too late to do anything about that as your son has heard all the stories already. One tack I might take would be to compare his dad's life as a teen with his. For example, his father didn't have a cell phone or a computer or an iPod. So you can tell him if he wants to be like his dad and drink beer as a teenager, he should give up all those items. It's not a trade that he's going to want to make, but you're going to have to let him know that if he gets caught, that trade won't be voluntary. It may not stop him, but it will make him think twice, I bet.

Keep Your Past to Yourself

While I encourage you to be open about at least some of the mistakes you make in front of your teen, I feel just the opposite when it comes to revealing the mistakes you made as a teen. If you brag to your children about your past exploits, you can be sure that these stories are going to come back to haunt you. If you catch your teen smoking pot, and she knows that you did it when you were in college, she's not going to listen to you when you tell her not to do it again. Whether or not she calls you a hypocrite to your face, she's certainly going to be thinking that. To avoid this type of situation, you have to keep your past somewhat buried. You can and should tell your children all the positive stories, but keep the negative ones to yourself.

Some of you may be thinking right about now, "If my kid asked me if I ever smoked pot, what do I say. Do I lie and say I didn't? If I dodge the question, won't she know I'm not being forthright with her, and figure I did?"

This whole line of questions goes back to my views on privacy. In my opinion, you need to keep parts of your life private from your children, at least until they become adults, and maybe even after that. If you've always told your children everything, and suddenly the question about pot or premarital sex or drinking arises, you're right, it's going to be hard to duck such a question. In that case, because you're doing it to protect your child, I would say to lie.

Now some of you might say that it's hypocritical, that because you did this or that and it didn't destroy your life that you shouldn't keep the truth about your past from your children. My argument goes back to what I said earlier, that you're a parent to your child, not a friend. One role of a parent is to be a counterbalance against peer pressure. If you give the green light to your child to smoke pot, then if your child had any hesitancy, you'll be adding to the peer pressure, not fighting it. If your daughter's boyfriend is pressuring her to have sex, and she knows that her mom had sex with her boyfriend at the same age, she's going to be more likely to give in, even if she's hesitant. If your daughter is adamant about having sex with her boyfriend, there's nothing much you can do to stop her. Where she needs your backup is if she's not sure what to do. And for that backup to be effective, she needs to believe not only your words, but your example. So in my opinion, it's better to whitewash your past to some extent so that you don't fall into the position of having to say, "Do as I say, not as I did."

Besides, no matter what you did as a teenager, the ramifications have changed. Because of social networking, your teen's exploits are going to wind up on the Web where they'll last forever. When you were a teen, the risk of catching AIDS if you had sex was nonexistent. Pot wasn't as potent as it is today. Getting a speeding ticket didn't go on a computerized list that could never be erased.

Since the dangers are greater, if it takes a white lie to keep your kids safe, then I say go ahead.

With Regard to the Future

Whatever peer pressure was telling your tween or teen to do yesterday, you can be sure it's slightly different today. Back in the day, a parent knew what to look out for because the rules for their teens were basically the same rules that had been set for them. But when you were a teen, you didn't have rules about what you could and couldn't put on your MySpace page. You couldn't take digital pictures of yourself in compromising situations and put them up where the entire world could see them. Sexual predators couldn't break into your room via your computer connection. You couldn't illegally download music and movies.

How do you keep up on all the latest dangers facing your children out there? You have to become technologically savvy. You need a basic understanding of the latest technological breakthroughs so that you can be on the lookout for the damage they can do in your home. I'll get more into specifics in Chapters 5 and 6, but because peer pressure compels your child to stay abreast of the latest technological advances, you have to do the same. An important part of your job as parent is to counteract peer pressure, but you can't do that if you don't know in what directions peer pressure may be pushing your child. So like it or not, set aside some time to do regular research on the dangers that are lurking in the shadows for your children that weren't there for you.

Sex Bracelets

Sex bracelets are an example of what I'm talking about. Sex bracelets are plastic jelly bracelets that come in different colors and supposedly wearing one signifies that you are willing to perform a certain sex act. Black is supposed to be for intercourse, blue for oral sex, purple for anal sex, and so on. Supposedly there are less blatant meanings too, like yellow could mean analingus or kiss. Now it's one thing for adults to wear them, but some teens and tweens have been wearing them also. I don't think that most tweens who might wear these really want to have sex, or fully understand what this is all about. The news media picked up on this and probably blew it out of all proportion, but nevertheless this story mixed with peer pressure could lead some tweens or teens into doing something they might later regret.

Of course if you've never heard of this and you have a teen or tween wearing one of these, then you're going to be oblivious to the potential danger. So I urge you to try to keep up, knowing that your kids will be one step ahead of you, but also knowing that one step isn't as dangerous as ten steps and around the corner.

For those of you who think that this concept is something new, did you know that back in the Victorian era, young ladies signaled their desires via their fans? If she was fanning herself quickly, it meant that she was available, but if she did it slowly, it meant that she was engaged. If she had the fan in front of her face using her right hand, it meant "come on, follow me," but if it was in her left hand, it meant "leave me alone." If she let her fan rest on her right cheek, it meant yes, while on her left cheek meant no, and if she drew the fan across her forehead, it meant "you are being watched." So you see the old French saying, *plus ca change, plus c'est la meme chose,* which means "the more things change the more things stay the same," remains valid to this day.

Maintaining Vigilance

As quickly as parents learn about one new fad, like the sex bracelets, teens find a new way to push the envelope. For example, there are clubs that cater to teens by having parties where no alcohol is sold. This sounds like a safe way for teens to hang out and be entertained. But one mother discovered to her horror, after telling her daughter that she could go to one of these, that a Web site advertising these parties featured pictures of young people having sex with their clothes on and dancers who bump and grind against each other up on a stage with practically no clothes on.

Kids find out about these parties through ads on MySpace or fliers posted around high schools. They may dress conservatively when they leave home, but when they arrive, they quickly strip off their outer garments revealing much scantier outfits underneath. There are girls as young as 13 in attendance sitting on their boyfriend's laps, as well as guys in their late teens and twenties. And even the fact that no alcohol is served and that there are guards to insure that no alcohol or drugs are consumed on premises (to protect those who are running these activities from prosecution) doesn't mean that many of those who go to these parties aren't wasted on either drugs or alcohol before they arrive.

So as a parent you have to maintain strict vigilance to make sure that your teen isn't involved in some activity that you never even dreamed existed. That's not always going to be easy, because teens can be very good at covering up what they're really doing, but if you're diligent, you can uncover the truth more often than not.

Hip-Hop

For the last 40 years new styles of music have become a part of peer pressure. For example, teens in the 1960s wore their hair longer because of the impact of the Beatles. In this decade one source of peer pressure has been hip-hop music, which features men saying awful things about women, while also featuring some women who aren't much better. While this style of music originated in the Black community, it has spread to the whole world.

Because of hip-hop, young men today are using expressions about women in public that would never have been used even in private before. Do these expressions have an effect on their behavior? I'm afraid so. After all, if you call women by vulgar names, after a while you're going to think of them that way as well. Can you stop your child from listening to such music? Only with great difficulty, given that teens can plug in earphones and you'll never really know what they're listening to. Better to assume that they at least are familiar with this type of music and to have a talk with them about it. Remind them that their mother is not a "ho" and that the mother of their future children is not going to be a "bitch" and that they had better understand that to even use words like that is demeaning to all women. And if you have a daughter, you have to give her the same message, because if young women didn't accept the use of this language around them, it would probably stop.

One could hope that this type of music will one day fade into the woodwork, but what replaces it could be worse. You, as a parent, can't control these external influences, but you can counteract them by making sure your children hear the opposite message. And the more you think they're hearing these negative ones, then the more work you'll have to do to give them positive ones. As I said, it's not easy, but you do have influence over them, and I urge you to use it as much as possible.

Madison Avenue

The ads that children see do have an influence over them too; otherwise, advertisers wouldn't spend the millions they do reaching out to young people. But today those ads are no longer limited to TV or in print media, but can also be seen over the Web, on cell phones, and just about anywhere else a teen's eyes might be focused. Just as with any other form of peer pressure, you have to be up on what your teen might be influenced by in order to counteract it. If your teen thinks that she has to wear a thong because it's fashionable, you have to explain to her the message that gives young men, because she may or may not understand it. So assume that she's innocent, even if she's way ahead of you. At least you'll get the opportunity to tell her how you feel.

The media also brings on the peer pressure of celebrities. If the latest craze among young female singers is to be seen by the paparazzi without any underwear, there's no doubt that will influence some young teens to doff their underwear. Again, it makes your job that much harder, though many of these teen idols tend to get themselves into trouble at some point, so perhaps your words of wisdom will get backed up by their stupidity.

Clothing

One of the lines of products that are heavily advertised to tweens and teens have to do with their appearance, especially clothing. I understand that teens want to adopt a certain appearance to show that they're hip, and while some styles may offend older people—like ripped clothing—they don't represent any particular danger. But when teens and teen girls dress very provocatively, that's where I draw the line.

I can't tell you whether these teenage girls know that they are arousing all the men around them when they walk around a mall half-naked, but the fact is they are. If they're wearing a bikini at the beach, that's appropriate, though I would certainly not let my daughter wear a thong; but away from the seashore, certain body parts need to be covered. I'm not saying they should wear a burqa, but they shouldn't be exposing too much skin because the message they're giving to every male nearby is "I'm available." Their aim may be to attract a particular teenage boy from school, but in fact they're causing many other men, for whom they have no interest, to have erections too. And while that is unfair to these strange men in the first place, it is also dangerous because one or more of these men might be a sexual predator who will take all this exposed flesh as a green light to approach her.

I realize that parents can't absolutely control what their teenage girls wear. For example, some schools may require that girls' skirts be just above the knee, but as soon as they're off the school grounds, every one of the students folds the top so that her skirt climbs one to six inches higher. And if a parent insists that a girl cover herself up when she leaves the house, she may uncover herself as soon as she turns the corner, or shows up at one of the clubs I mentioned earlier.

Teenage girls feel the need to be "hot." They don't want to walk around being ignored by male teens but want to be looked at. What they don't understand is that young men will still look at them if they're wearing less revealing outfits, but they will also have more respect for them. Street prostitutes get looked at, they even have sex with lots of men, but none of these men would want to marry one of them. Pierre remembers a girl in college who wore a ton of makeup because it made people stare at her. The sad part was, they were looking at her because she looked like a freak, not because they found her attractive.

Your job as a parent is to explain to your daughter the difference between being admired and leered at. Peer pressure, the way all her friends are dressing, is definitely going to have a major effect on how she looks when she's out of your sight, but if you can get her to tone down the sexual content of the image she's projecting even by a fraction, that would be progress. And as I've said before, while she may sigh and raise her eyebrows while you're explaining to her that how she dresses is important, she will be getting the message nevertheless.

A Hard Job

I understand that after a while you might feel overwhelmed having to fight these various sorts of pressures that have a tremendous influence over your children, but what you have to remember is that your influence is even stronger. You've raised them since they were born, they have an innate love for you, and they see you constantly and imitate you. So rather than being the imitator and mimicking your teens in dress and looks in order to make yourself seem younger, which is only going to add to the pressure they're under, you have to show them what it's like to be an adult. By setting the proper example, you can counteract much of the peer pressure that is all around your teens, but you have to make a conscious effort to do so, and you can't ease up, because the pressure never ceases. If you get even a small tattoo on your ankle, for example, you can bet that your teen will get a larger one somewhere else. So I would encourage you to resist that urge, not because tattoos are inherently bad, but because of what it will do to the image you project to your children.

For Girls

Children often break into cliques, and while it's no fun to be rejected by a group of girls, there are also dangers to watch out for upon acceptance. Being part of an in-group requires conforming to the group's rules. This can severely increase the power of peer pressure. If your daughter is on the cusp of being accepted into one of these groups, she might be pushed into doing things that she knows are bad just to make sure that she either gains or maintains her acceptance. If your daughter is already part of the in-crowd, then rather than sitting back and taking pride in this fact, you have to become extra vigilant. If, for example, having oral sex has been decided to be one of the integral rules of acceptance, the pressure on your daughter to engage in this activity will increase tremendously. It won't matter whether she wants to do it or enjoys doing it. Like binge drinking, smoking, or sporting a tattoo, oral sex may be an activity she is forced to engage in to remain part of the group.

You may think, and certainly your daughter will do everything she can to make you believe, that your job is to help her maintain her standing among her friends. If it means buying some new clothes or a particular cell phone that are within your budget, then that may be all right. But if it seems that your daughter is under a lot of pressure because of her group standing, then you must ask questions, and you may have to don the role of "meanie" in order to make certain that this type of peer pressure isn't having a negative effect. She may "hate" you, but in the long run she'll thank you because while she'll know that what she's being forced to do is wrong, she won't have the will power to leave the group on her own. Just the fact that she can blame you will make it a lot easier on her.

For Boys

The parents of girls all worry about the risks of an unintended pregnancy but the parents of boys are usually less concerned, and a teenage boy will pick up on that attitude, taking it as a message that he can go ahead and have sex because at least he can't get pregnant. For that reason, it's up to his parents to make sure that he understands that if he causes a pregnancy, he's not going to get away with shirking his responsibilities. He has to understand that you, his parents, are not going to just step in and make the situation go away, but that his life will be seriously affected. While you may not be able to stop yourself from giving the subconscious message that having a son makes sex less risky, that means you must make a conscious effort to let your son know the consequences.

CHAPTER 5

Computers and
Social Networking

WHETHER OR NOT you're as computer savvy as your children, you probably do use computers for e-mail and doing Web searches, and there's a good chance that you're like many adults who spend hours on them at work every day. So I'm going to assume that all of you reading this book have at least a working knowledge of computers. If that's not the case, then you have even more work to do than everyone else because if you don't have a working knowledge of computers, then you'll have an even more difficult time keeping tabs on your children.

Computers have changed the way we live and work, making many tasks easier—because one person can now handle the duties of two or three people—and allowing us to do things we could never have done before. But they also make many of us work a lot harder, which means rather than spending more time with our kids, we end up spending less. And as a result, we know less about what they're up to. And since computers allow them to do more, in terms of exploring our world in so many new ways, problems can develop.

In this chapter I'm going to cover one aspect of computers and your teen, and that's social networking. There are issues of sexual content involved in social networking and social utilities, but I'll deal with those in the next chapter.

Social networks have always existed. You've heard the term *pecking order*, I'm sure, and that refers to the social networking of chickens. Chickens and every other animal in the world follow certain social rules, and so it shouldn't come as a surprise that we human animals do, too. What we're going to examine in this chapter are the ways in which computers have changed the way our children interact socially.

Friendship used to be a somewhat exclusive relationship. In schools, kids would break into cliques, and while everyone might want to be friends with the most popular kids, they'd keep their list of friends to a minimum. A child in school might know lots of other boys and girls, but the child's list of close friends would be much smaller, limited to maybe half a dozen or so. It made sense because how many people could you interact with on a regular basis? Computers have turned that model upside down.

I suppose the tectonic shift began with AOL's Instant Messenger service, or AIM. Suddenly it became important to have as many friends on your "Buddy List" as possible. Instead of limiting access, tweens and teens were maximizing their social network. If you didn't have at least 100 Buddies, something was the matter with you. And since you were trying to increase the size of your list, excluding people became counterproductive. To prove yourself the most popular person, you had to have the most extensive Buddy List instead of having an exclusive circle of friends. Of course no one could actually conduct instant-messengering chats with that many people at once, but AIM changed the direction of where the definition of "popularity" was heading. Once less became more, it was really only a matter of time before other Web sites figured out how to take advantage of this trend.

Another factor that changed the way young people interacted occurred when cell phones, which to every teen had become a must-have, all came equipped with built-in digital cameras. What was the fun of taking all these digital pictures if you couldn't share them? Again, the social networking or social utility sites easily slid in to fill that gap. The first one was Classmates.com, which began in 1995. Today the big ones are MySpace and Facebook, but there are dozens nipping at their heels, such as Friendsfusion, Friendster, Intellectconnect, LiveJournal, Tagworld, and Xanga. (There are even social networking sites for young children, like Webkinz. That age group is not in the scope of this book, but you can be sure if pretweens are into social networking, they'll be doing it even more once they're older, unless someone invents something else.) Since new ones pop up every day, trying to keep up with the regular changes in popularity of these sites will be included in your learning curve.

While cell phones at one time took only still pictures, now they can also shoot video (like any digital camera). So now in addition to having to worry about having embarrassing pictures posted on the Web, it can also be videos, which would include sound as well. YouTube offers the biggest collection of videos, but there are others, and videos can also be posted to MySpace and Facebook.

There are hundreds of other social networking sites that are not aimed at teens, per se, and theoretically, there's nothing wrong with a social networking site. They use an existing technology to help people, both young and old, stay in contact. But at the time we're writing this, MySpace has just deleted 29,000 convicted sex offenders from their site. Since they have over 70 million users, that's not as large a percentage as it first appears. But with over 600,000 convicted sex offenders, and a whole lot more who've not been caught, it's obvious that the lure of having so many young people offering up personal information is one that is going to attract the wrong type of people, and maybe attract them to your child.

While you're panicking, let's look at your options. One is to do nothing. If you were concerned enough to pick up this book to prepare yourself to deal with your teen, then I know that's not an option for you. At the other extreme, you could forbid your tween or teen from posting a personal page on one of these sites. To a teen, that option would be akin to instant death since according to the latest data, 96% of teens use these sites. One reason that this rate is so high is that the makers of these sites don't want people to take away the bait without getting hooked: They force anyone who wants to see someone else's page to become a member and set up his or her own page. So the consequence of forbidding your child from having a page of his or her own would be that your teen would not be able to participate in this form of communication at all. You know how kids are prone to say, "But Mom, everyone's doing it"? Well, in this case it would be true. To your teen, not having a page on a social networking site would be socially devastating, and I bet that he or she would find a way around it. Some libraries are already having a problem with teens tying up their computers to go on these sites. Though these are probably mostly young people who don't have a computer at home, I'm sure that some are teens who've been forbidden from using their home computer for this purpose. As with other taboos, once they've disobeyed their parents, they'd be without any boundary lines. In fact, assuming that such a teen didn't have a lot of time to work on his site because the home computer was off limits, forcing him to use another computer at a library, cybercafe, or friend's house to launch the site, he might post content that was extra shocking to draw attention to it. He'd justify it to himself by saying, "Well, I don't have the time to really work on it," but in the back of his mind he'd be saying, "Mom and Dad won't ask to check my site since I'm not supposed to have one in the first place, so I can put anything I want on my site." In other words, I wouldn't be surprised if such a total ban backfired altogether. So that leaves you with another option that I think is best: coming up with a set of rules that will allow your teen to participate in the action while also protecting him, as best you can.

Obviously, the first step, no matter what your ultimate plan, is to explain the dangers to your child. If you've told your child not to take candy from strangers, that was probably the extent of the message you gave; you weren't going to explain what a sexual predator was to a five-year-old. Now, however, you have to give your teen more of an explanation. These predators aren't going to announce themselves. Most will pretend that they are fellow teens. That means that your teen is going to have to be especially savvy to spot one. Therefore, your teen has to understand what she's up against.

Sidebar: Sexual Predators

You might think that all sexual predators are the same, but they're not. There are basically two types. One type is called a *pedophile*. Pedophiles have a strong attraction toward having sex with prepubescent youngsters. While I'm not excusing their behavior, to some extent they may not be able to help themselves. According to some studies, just as a heterosexual is attracted to people of the opposite sex and a homosexual to people of the same sex, a pedophile is attracted to prepubescent youngsters. Sexual offenders, on the other hand, may not prefer to have sex with young people, but they do so because of situational reasons. For example, most cases of father-daughter incest are situational, that is to say, the father (or uncle or grandfather or older cousin) might prefer to have sex with an adult, but for whatever reasons, no adult partner is available and so they turn to a young, nearby female relative. What all this means is that some of the online sexual predators are pedophiles, looking to have sex with young people because that's what attracts them, while others are just trolling around for easy prey. I know that you don't want your children to encounter either type, but it's always good to know as much about the enemy as possible.

One characteristic of sexual predators is patience. They know that if they try to convince a teen or tween the first time they communicate online to engage in any sexual activity that their victim is going to shut down the connection. So instead they try to befriend the child slowly. They'll be sympathetic to their complaints. They may even send them gifts. This process has been labeled *grooming*. Your children need to be made aware of this so that if a "friend" that they met online suddenly starts bringing up sex, they have to immediately realize the true goal of this person.

By the way, they shouldn't start playing detective. Some teens are going to think that if they can trap this person that they'll be a hero. They might even agree to meet them with that goal in mind. (This attitude might be fueled by TV shows that do exactly that.) Make sure that your teens understand that these predators are dangerous. If your teens are sure that they are communicating with a sexual predator, then you should contact the proper authorities. They'll be able to deal with the situation safely.

Sexual predators don't have to come into direct contact with your child in order to be dangerous. Some convince young people that they will harm their parents unless they do as they're told, which may mean taking pictures or videos of themselves in the nude and while performing sex acts and sending them to the predator, who in turn will probably share them with others with similar tastes.

It's Not Just Sexual Predators

While sexual predators are clearly one danger, there are others. For example if your teen posts news about an upcoming family vacation, he's also announcing to anyone who's reading that there's going to be an empty house at your address, perfect for robbing. And if your teen has enough personal information about herself online, then she's open to identity theft. So you see, there's more than one type of criminal out to use social networking sites to commit their dirty deeds.

As I've said several times, I'm not a believer in using fear as a way of changing behavior, mostly because it doesn't work. So I am definitely not suggesting that you try to scare your teen from going on MySpace or Facebook because I know you're going to fail. I also realize that most of the sexual innuendos that your teen may encounter on these sites will be from fellow teens, many of whom they know. Flirting is important at that age, and while the nature of flirting has certainly changed—being a lot more sexual these days than when a young lady would merely drop her handkerchief—such social interactions make good practice sessions. Teens gain needed experience by flirting with each other for the future, when they'll be taking the next steps to having real relationships. So not only can't you stop some sexual interplay from taking place in any form of communications where young men and women are involved, but you shouldn't. A teen left in social isolation is actually more vulnerable to be taking advantage of later in life.

While there is real danger out there from adults who prey on young people, the odds of any one teen falling prey to such a person is small, and the need to be part of the social network of teens is large. Your duty as a parent is to make sure that your child understands the dangers, while allowing him the freedom to explore this world. It's very similar to driving. Of course you're scared every time your newly licensed teen takes the keys to the family car, but you know that he has to practice driving to become good at it, and so you take a deep breath and say, "Be careful," for the thousandth time to his back as he goes out the door. Now the potential dangers of driving are a lot higher than going on the Internet, so you have to react accordingly. If you get hysterical about every danger your teenager faces, he's going to just tune you out. You need to give a reasonable explanation for your fears, and you need to remind him occasionally to make sure that he doesn't forget the message, but mostly you just have to pray that nothing happens.

Were you surprised that MySpace had to remove 29,000 sex offenders from its lists? I was, and I'm sure you were too, whether you read it here first or had seen the story in the papers. I'm also sure that your teen is going to be somewhat impressed with that number. That's why I don't think you have to go overboard with demonstrating the dangers. If your daughter is old enough to be using MySpace or Facebook, then she will, in all probability, be able to assimilate enough of the message of the dangers from sexual offenders to protect herself. But teens do tend to forget such warnings, so be sure to repeat it every now and again

Vulnerable Teens

There are some teens, however, who are going to be more vulnerable than others, and sexual predators know this. They understand that most of the teens they are going to approach will either spot them as a fake or simply ignore their propositions. After all, most teens are interested in interacting with their friends, not strangers. What these predators hope to find, however, is a teen who for whatever reason has low self-esteem and not many friends, and who is looking for attention and so will take the bait. As a parent, your job is to accurately identify your teen's position on the scale of vulnerability. If your teen has plenty of friends, if her cell phone is always ringing, if he's always hanging out with his buddies, if she has at least one close friend that she can confide in, then I think you can be a lot more relaxed when it comes to the dangers lurking on the Web. But if your teen is a loner, if she spends Friday and Saturday nights locked in her bedroom, and especially if she spends a lot of her free time on her computer, then you must be a lot more vigilant. She may say she's online with her friends, but if those "friends" never make themselves apparent in other ways, then you have to ask yourself if they're people she knows in real life, or only on the Web. If they're people she only knows from the Web, then that means that basically she's chatting with strangers. Most of them are going to be other teens who share similar interests and may be similarly lonely, but every once in a while, one is going to be adult predator posing as a teen. And if he's any good at what he does, then she's in danger.

The main problem with such a teen is not the computer. She may have low self-esteem, or something happened that pushed her away from having a set of friends. Yes, such a teen is vulnerable to online predators, but she's also vulnerable to having other problems as well. In this instance, don't blame the computer but be thankful that it allowed you to see that your child has a social problem. Reach out to her to see if you can help. Maybe talk to her teachers to see if they have seen any evidence of problems she may be having in school. Talk to her school counselor. Offer her private counseling, which she may willingly accept if she's unhappy.

If her online friends are her lifeline to the outside world, you'll have to be careful of how you handle the issue of predators. Make sure that she's hiding behind some alias and isn't giving out her real name and address. There's a good chance she is going to be very protective of her online world, but that doesn't mean she won't listen to you. And as long as she doesn't actually come into physical contact with anyone, she's still safe. If you try to cut her off, then she might do something stupid out of rebellion, so be vigilant but don't take any action unless you see evidence of actual danger.

Although the teens I've just described are more vulnerable than others, don't think that if your child is not a loner that he or she is not at risk. The first child murdered by a sexual predator that she met on the Web was an honors student, cocaptain of the cheerleading team, and very popular. So while it's true that certain children are more vulnerable, it doesn't mean that the king and queen of the prom aren't also at risk.

Join a Social Network

If you're not a member of one of these social networks, my advice is to join one—not so that you can spend hours posting all your private information to share with the entire world, but so that you have a better understanding of how they work. Since you drive a car, you know to tell your teen to be careful of the blind spot when changing lanes, but if you know nothing about any of these social networks, then that places you at a disadvantage when it comes to understanding the potential dangers of online activities. I'm not saying you have to become an expert, but you should know the basics so that at least you know the proper terms and can have a discussion with your teen without sounding like a know-nothing. And the more you know, the better you'll be able to ask questions. Most teens don't like to lie, but they quickly become very good at avoiding giving you the real answer to a question by only answering part of it. Ask a teen what time he'll be home, and he won't give you an exact time, rather saying, "Later," so that you can't pin him down. It's up to you then to set the time, and very clearly. If you're clueless when it comes to these sites, then your teen is going to have an easier time dodging your questions by giving you half answers, which is why you need to know the whole story.

In fact, you can ask your teen to help you put together your page. I'm not saying this is an ideal way of bonding, but it will show your teen how serious you are about the potential dangers since you're taking the time to learn as much as you can. And with a teen acting as a tutor, you'll gain a lot of knowledge quickly. Then you can do some further exploring to make sure that there wasn't anything your instructor "accidentally" forgot to tell you.

You can also insist that your teen show you his or her pages on MySpace or Facebook. If you do, and your teen doesn't throw a tantrum, don't be overly critical when you're staring at the computer screen. You're looking to make sure that there are no nude pictures of your teen and nothing that will lead a predator back to your house. If the language is a little dicey or whatever, shut your eyes. If you come down too hard, your teen will just clean up that space, and start another one that he or she won't let you see. (As long as there are free e-mails available, such as Hotmail, Yahoo Mail, Gmail, it's easy for anyone, including a teen, to have more than one e-mail address and therefore have more than one social networking persona.) One thing about his site that you should check together is his privacy settings. If he's limiting the people who can get on his page to only his close friends, then he's obviously a lot safer than if he's left himself open to a much larger group.

When looking at photographs or videos that are posted, don't be content to examine them to see whether they're too racy or

not. If there's anything in the background that can help a criminal identify your teen, then that photo should not be put on the site. Obvious culprits would be a house number or license plate. But one area that your teen has to guard against is the name of his or her school. Many of these sites use schools to group people, so a predator goes online posing as a student at a particular school in order to learn information about the other students. So the name of your teen's school, as well as other ways to identify it, like a team name or mascot, must be kept off the page. And remember, by zooming in, it's possible to see details, so you have to look at the picture closely, not just give it a quick overview. Part of the fun for these predators is the hunt, and playing detective by looking for even small clues is what they do best.

I guess I shouldn't avoid the obvious but state that your teen's real name, address, phone, cell phone, date of birth, social security number, and calendar of activities are all facts that should never be put up on one of these sites. Your teen may think this information is only being seen by friends, but instead he or she has to adopt the mindset that the entire world is scrutinizing every word and image.

You should also teach your child not to automatically click on attachments that come in e-mails. In the first place, they could contain a virus that would destroy your computer's hard drive. But in addition, some stranger could send all sorts of horrific photos or stories to your child this way. So tell your child to always stop and think before clicking anything that comes attached to an e-mail. If your child doesn't know the person, the best thing to click is the delete key to erase the e-mail, thereby completely protecting himself from any potential danger.

Invading Their Privacy

As you already know, I'm very much in favor of maintaining everyone's privacy, both adults and teens, but I also understand that sometimes safety comes before privacy, especially when it comes to children. Some teens may not care that you look at their MySpace or Facebook page any time you want. They can make you a "friend" and then you'll have as much access as anyone else. You can also ask for their password.

If a request to see a teen's social networking pages is a first, you might consider making an appointment. If you're not going to see the pages until the next day, your teen is going to clean up her Facebook pages. How much she removes will depend on how much she has on there that she's ashamed to show you. This is a way of protecting her privacy, like knocking before you enter her room. True, you won't know what she removed, but if she knows that from now on you're going to want to inspect her site from time to time, then she'll probably be more careful of what she puts onto it, and that's the point of your wanting to look at it in the first place. Since teens are prone to exaggerate, the material she removes might not have been real, but only some fabrications, so the danger might not be as big as you might have presumed had you seen this material. WiredSafety provides help, information, and education to Internet and mobile device users of all ages. This site helps victims of cyberabuse ranging from online fraud, cyberstalking, and child safety, to hacking and malicious code attacks. They also help parents with issues, such as MySpace and cyberbullying. On the other hand, if you demand to see her pages right this minute, and you do find objectionable material, then you'll be faced with a crisis, which may lead her to hide her pages so that you can't see them.

Of course some teens are going to balk at any such inspection entirely. For teens to demand privacy is entirely natural. It's part of the breaking away process. On the other hand, a MySpace page isn't like a paper diary because the whole point is that other people can read it, so as their parent you have a right and a duty to see what they're doing on this very public space. Finding a happy medium is what can be challenging.

Obviously, you can force a teen to reveal all, or else cut off his computer privileges, but as I said earlier, that could defeat the purpose because he'll be able to find other ways of using another computer or identity and then you'll have no control over that space at all. For parents who are caught in such a trap—where they want to keep track of what their teen is doing online but their teen refuses access—I'd be remiss if I didn't tell you about some options that will allow you to find out what your teen is actually doing on her computer, whether she wants you to or not.

The first thing a parent should do is to Google their child. *To Google* means to use the search engine Google—though you could use another one, such as Yahoo—to look something up. Type your child's name into Google and see what comes up. If the first thing you see is an article in the high school paper announcing that your daughter won some honor, then you'll smile (especially if she forgot to tell you). But on the other hand, you may find something that you don't want to see as well. (Hint: to limit your search, put your child's name in quotation marks—"john smith"—so you'll only see the results for him and not for every Smith in the world. If your child has a nickname, use that as well.) And if you've never Googled your own name, try that as well. You never know what someone might have put online about you.

Your second line of defense are the programs and devices that come under the category of *key loggers*. These allow you to see from a separate computer what your teen is doing on your home computer, or if she has a personal computer, on that computer. I haven't reviewed all the various software, since they're all pretty similar, but I did look fairly closely at one, which is software that comes loaded onto a small portable USB drive and is called SnoopStick. When you plug the device into a computer's USB port, it automatically loads its software, thus allowing you to see exactly what your child (or spouse or employee for that matter) is doing on that computer without having any idea that every keystroke is being recorded. Then you plug the SnoopStick into the USB port of the computer you're going to do your snooping from, and download the software. While at this computer—your office computer, for example— you can be overseeing what your teenager is doing on your home computer. You can see which Web sites are visited, view entire IM conversations, find out who has sent your teen e-mails, and even see exactly what was on your computer screen at a given moment by taking "snapshots." Not only can you see what's happening at the moment, you can also see what was happening prior to your logging on. Not much escapes the SnoopStick, and so you'll know pretty much what your child is doing when you're not physically looking over his or her shoulder.

If you want to do more than just spy—meaning take actual intervention—you can announce yourself, and tell your child to get off a particular Web site, or else you can shut the Internet connection off, surreptitiously so that it will appear that there is a network problem, rather than reveal that you were behind it. The SnoopStick can even contact you automatically if your teen is on a specifically forbidden site.

As mentioned above, you don't have to do all this snooping behind your child's back. You can announce yourself the first time you catch your son on a site he's not supposed to be on, or you can tell him in advance that you'll be watching. If you feel at all guilty about spying on your children, the latter approach should satisfy any ethical concerns you may have. Of course, if your teen knows he's being watched, he may be able to outwit some of your ability to see what he's doing, such as using an online e-mail account rather than the one given to you by your Internet provider, but he won't be able to completely disable the system, assuming you follow the directions when first setting it up.

I know that I'm supposed to be giving you advice, but here's a case when I'm going to take a pass. No parent should take an invasion of privacy of this sort lightly. I would hope that you would only consider snooping like this if you had a good reason to suspect that your teen was acting inappropriately, and so only you could judge whether this sort of spying was the right approach or not. If you caught your teen on a forbidden site, one alternative would be to just cancel your Internet service altogether, which would do away with the problem, though I know that these days, that would cause problems both for the rest of the family and even for your teen, who may be required to do research for schoolwork.

I Heard The News Today, Oh Boy

In the previous chapter on peer pressure, I wrote about the concept that actions taken by teens, or anyone for that matter, can now live on the Internet forever and that teens must understand this new paradigm when deciding which types of behavior to engage in and which to skip. Certainly one of the ways that teens are most vulnerable to this effect is via these social networking sites. An instant message or e-mail sent to a friend about a prank could be saved on a hard drive, but most likely it won't be broadcast far and wide, even though the potential is there for the recipient to blast it out to hundreds. But material put up on a social networking site is automatically going to be seen by lots of people. And just as you're more likely to be infected by a sexually transmitted disease if you sleep around with more people, it is more likely that news you don't want spread far and wide, will be, if your page on one of these social networking or social utility sites is popular.

I've given you this message twice now, and maybe you're already saying to yourself, "OK, Dr. Ruth, I get it." If you, in turn, pound away at your teen about this, you can be certain that they will also feel exasperated at being told the same thing again and again. But on the other hand, if you don't constantly remind them, the message will be like the garbage that never gets put out without you asking several times. Young people are in the process of breaking away, and sometimes it's hard for them to distinguish between appropriate times for rebelling and inappropriate times. This is one of those messages that you're going to have to raise from time to time, just as you're going to have to reissue the warning about not putting anything inappropriate on their social networking sites, since many teens have a tendency to believe that there is an expiration date on the orders given by their parents.

Cyberbullying

So far I've been dealing with problems caused outside your child's network of friends, but sometimes it's someone your teen knows that can be the source of of your teen's suffering. It used to be that bullies had to find their victims either in the neighborhood playground or in the school yard. Home was a safety zone. But in today's wired world, that's no longer the case. Now a child can receive threats electronically, and such attacks can be just as frightening as physical ones.

All children tease each other. That's never going to stop. Being teased is annoying but it's not frightening. When teasing becomes scary, that's when the line has been crossed into bullying. So if your teen is receiving messages that are causing concern and even fear, or is sending such messages, then it's become a case of cyberbullying.

Cyberbullying is preventable to some degree because it's possible to block electronic communication be it via e-mail, instant messenger, or chat from any particular individual or group. But cyberbullying may be one aspect of actual physical bullying so that a child won't dare block the access of the bully for fear of the potential physical response when the bully is encountered outside. And if the bully is saying nasty things about your son or daughter in his own MySpace page, for example, then that's also out of your child's control to stop. A child's reputation can be very fragile and so this type of activity can be very damaging.

The one difference between electronic bullying and the in-your-face type is that it leaves a trail, and thus proof of the activity. If your child is a victim too frightened to report the bullying, then this proof is useless. But if your child comes to you and complains, you'll have ammunition with which to fight back. So the key is to find out whether or not your child is the victim of some bully, or group of bullies. Certainly you should ask your child from time to time whether everything is all right, and particularly if you notice any differences in behavior. Any time a student's grades drop dramatically, you should look at that as a sign of something being amiss. But changes don't have to be negative in order to be a sign of trouble. You might think that spending a lot less time on the computer than before is a positive change for your son, but if the reason behind this abrupt switch is that a cyberbully is constantly e-mailing threats, then obviously this reduction of computer time is a sign of trouble. So keep your eyes peeled and pay attention to any changes in behavior you see.

In cases of cyberbullying between students, some school administrations are willing to help and some are not, afraid that they'll be infringing on the bullies' rights of free speech. That, of course, is nonsense, and if you run into such an attitude, fight back. It will be a lot easier to have success if school officials are involved than if you have to confront the bully, or his or her parents, on your own. Of course if the evidence is strong enough, you can also go to the police. It's best if you can stop the bullying without resorting to this last approach, but if it's the only option left to you, don't automatically consider it too strong a response. After all, the psychological damage of bullying on your child can be quite serious.

Cyberbullying is a growing phenomena. That makes sense because as any one individual is connected to more and more people via the Web, it means the odds of running into a bully, or someone who has some other personality disorder, are higher. Bullying, in general, is not something that you should ignore. Studies have shown that bullies grow up having a higher risk of mental disorders, and the victims have an elevated risk of anxiety disorders when they grow up. So this isn't just kids being kids. If someone is being bullied or acting like a bully in your family, you must take action.

A Word About Schools

When you get right down to it, your teen's school should be more involved in social networking altogether, though most schools are not. Sixty percent of teens report that one of the topics of their social networking is school and school work. So schools are remiss in staying away from social networking as this could be an important learning tool, if used properly. For example, not that long ago parents would decry the fact that their kids didn't write. Then along came all this social networking and their kids are writing more than any generation before. The use of shortcuts and emoticons is creeping into the classroom, which some teachers find rightfully appalling, but the best way to deal with this issue is to find ways of working with teens with regard to social networking sites, as well as chatting, IMing, and e-mailing, rather than just criticizing them for it. Yet most schools have rules forbidding students from accessing social networking during school hours. If the students have no access while they're at school, the school has no influence over what they are writing. I'm not saying that finding the best way of using social networking in schools is going to be easy, but it won't be discovered at all if social networking is kept at arms length.

Starting Early

If you have teens using computers, they've probably been using them for some time. Hopefully, you laid down some ground rules and took some precautions when they first began. But in case you didn't, here are some other ideas about controlling computer use that may be helpful, though I can predict if you suddenly impose them with regard to an older teen, you're going to be in for a minor revolution.

The first is computer placement. If the computer is in a den or kitchen area, where people passing by can easily see what's on the screen, then it's harder for a son or daughter to hide material that's not fit for parental consumption, If there's more than one child in the house, and more than one computer, then it might be a piece of educational equipment that they each have in their room. For teens, who might require more peace and quiet while doing home-work, that's even understandable, but also riskier. If that's the case, then you might have a rule that says that if they're on the com-puter, they must keep the door to their room open (which in turn may mean that they have to keep the volume of any music down or off altogether).

The other tool that many parents use is a contract about com-puter use. Just about every parent has heard the words, "You never said that" or "I didn't understand that." Since we're talking about real potential dangers here, it may be better to head those phrases off at the pass by making your child sign a contract that very spe-cifically outlines what he or she can and cannot do with regard to the computer. I've included a generic contract in Appendix A of this book. You can use it as is or adapt it in any way you see fit, if you don't think it suits your needs exactly. It doesn't have to pass muster in a court of law; it just has to help you enforce the set of rules you've laid down for your household.

And if you'd like to learn more about this whole issue, Appen-dix B includes a list of sites that you might find helpful. As you know, Web sites change regularly, so please excuse me if any that I've given are no longer up and running at the time you look them up.

For Boys

Young men, and even older men, have always bragged. Be it the fish story about the "one that got away" or the locker room talk about what happened the night before with some young lady or how much was drunk at a fraternity party, bragging just seems to be something that men do. Bragging to your buddies may be fun, but as we've seen in this chapter, bragging online could have a long-term, negative effect.

It's going to be very tempting to your son to use his social networking sites to brag and exaggerate. After all, if he does that with his buddies when they're together, why would he stop when he's online? So it's up to you to make him. He's not going to be able to differentiate between the bragging he does in person and the bragging he does online. You can easily see how difficult it could be to act differently with your friends online than you do in person. But the differences between the real world and the cyber world are something that you're going to have to drill into his head. The world isn't going to get any less interconnected by computers, but instead we're all going to become more and more connected. Your son has to understand that the consequences of using those connections to brag could be quite costly in the long run.

For Girls

"Sugar and spice and everything nice" may once have described little girls, but these days that's not always true. However, a girl's reputation is still very important. Young men may like to have sex with young women who "put out" but the double standard remains and when it comes to settling down, the girl who is known as a slut will have problems finding a man who'll stick by her.

It's unfair that there's a double standard, but unfair or not, it still exists. While boys may increase their standing by bragging, a girl who lets it be known that she's had sex with many partners will pay a price. Your daughter has to be made to understand this, so that she keeps certain aspects of her life private. A MySpace or Facebook page is not a diary that is under lock and key. She has to learn how to censor what she puts down or else she may end up regretting it. Of course you may not know much if anything about your daughter's sex life, and so you'll have to speak in generalities. But you must make sure that she understands the overall point that when she's online, she has to be as conservative as possible.

CHAPTER 6

Computers and Sex

THIS CHAPTER COULD be a very short one. You might imagine that all it really needs to say is this: If you have children at home, load software into your computer that will block all sites having to do with sex. As you can see, it's longer than that and for several reasons. The first is that I would be remiss not to explain the dangers so that you understand why it is important to consider having such software or taking other precautions. But you also have to know that software is not enough, because the effects of porn are going to reach your child whether or not even one erotic image ever appears on your computer monitor. And that fact leads to another thought to consider with regard to teens, especially older teens, which is that blocking everything having to do with sex might not be appropriate. For example, my Web site, www.drruth.com, would end up being blocked, and my site, like many others, provides valuable information. Teens can get answers to their questions on such sites, answers that could save their lives or save them from an unintended pregnancy. Trust me, I know this because of the type of questions I get. There are many sexually active teens out there who either never got that birds and bees talk or weren't listening. For example, teens are always asking about the pull-out method, which is not a good way of preventing pregnancy, though too many don't know that. So even if you already have such software on your computer, don't skip this chapter because not only will you learn some new information, but hopefully you'll also have a better understanding of what you're really up against and how to combat it.

What's Available

Maybe I should have titled this section "What's Not Available," because there's nothing having to do with sex that is not covered on the Web, including some fetishes that I'd never heard of that are given full coverage on many Web sites. (You may well have heard of foot fetishists and latex fetishists, but balloon fetishists?) What makes this problematic for teens is that not only is so much of this material available, it's also available for free. There are many sites that cost money, but I bet most teens won't pay money for this x-rated material. Why should they when there are free areas on all these sites that are often quite extensive? So even if a teen doesn't have a credit card on which to charge the entry fee, he doesn't really need one to get quite a view of what's inside.

One reason that these sites use credit cards is supposedly to prevent minors from entering, but all you have to do to look at the free material is swear you're 18. Some sites are a little harder to get on, but there are so many that are so easy that to speak about barriers is ludicrous. And I'm not even sure that the hunting aspect—the way to get the forbidden fruit without the adults who run these sites knowing—isn't part of the lure.

I am not against erotica per se. And one could even argue that it wouldn't be a bad trade-off, giving teens access to erotica that would assist them in masturbation—and would, in turn, keep them from engaging in sex with other teens, thus protecting them from the accompanying dangers of STDs and unintended pregnancies. I would certainly agree with that if all a teen could look at were pictures of naked women, a la *Playboy*. (Of course if your teen happens to be gay, there are no shortages of pictures of naked men as well, not to mention sites that cater to lesbians and transgendered people also.) Your values might differ, but I see nothing wrong with a teenage boy having some copies of *Playboy* hidden away in his room. However, the Web isn't limited to what's inside the covers of *Playboy*; not by any means.

To my way of thinking, and I hope to yours, sex is something that should be explored slowly. Holding hands brings with it distinct pleasures, and I believe that if two young people can remain at that stage for a time before they begin to explore the next stage, say kissing, that it would be wonderful for both of them. I think the longer each stage is drawn out, the better, because let's face it, when you've advanced to the next stage, you don't appreciate the previous stages quite as much. But for too many young people the idea of lingering at one stage is quaint, and it ends up becoming a rush to the finish line, so to speak. Since you have an entire lifetime ahead of you, why not indulge in a period where you still get a thrill from holding hands? Or putting your arms around each other? But as we know, teens are always in a rush. And at the start of the twenty-first century, as compared to the middle of the twentieth and before, many teens progress much too fast. As we already discussed, even if they're willing to wait to have intercourse, they go ahead and have oral sex, and maybe anal sex as well. The reason I'm bringing this up here is that some of this mad dash to experience every possible aspect of sex arises from teens having seen very explicit material on porn sites which gives them the idea that such behavior is "normal."

Does the violence we see on screen make us more violent? I don't know the answer to that for certain, but most of us don't engage in violent behavior regularly, so even if there is a bit of a push in that direction, seeing a violent movie or two or playing a violent video game is not necessarily enough to make most of us go out and commit an act of violence. But while violence is not something we all experience, we're all sexual creatures, have sexual desires, and eventually do engage in sex. So without a doubt what we see on screen that is related to sex, whether that be in a movie theater, on a television set, or on a computer monitor, definitely does affect our later behavior. And I have no doubt that for teens to have seen so many images of people engaging in oral sex, for example, did in turn influence their real-life behavior. Seeing so many shaved genitals has also influenced that aspect of their appearance, and seeing actions like "facials," where the man ejaculates onto the face of the woman, has also caused a lot of young men to expect his partner to accept this particular act, which to me is so demeaning to women.

If you're wondering how I know what's going on in the bedrooms and back seats of cars around the country, it's simple: I get e-mails. Obviously, these aren't scientific surveys, but you can be sure if some teens are e-mailing me about such issues, then tens of thousands of others are encountering the same problems. So while it may be hard for you to think of your little girl, who not so long ago was your little baby, being pressured by her boyfriend to undergo a "facial," it may well have already happened, or soon will. And if she's even contemplating it, something that I imagine would never have even crossed your mind when you were her age, then the reason is that it is an act commonly depicted in pornographic material. I'm not saying that she's necessarily seen this, or that if she had, would find it appealing. But if the young men she hangs around with have, then there's a good chance that she'll come under pressure to do it.

I'm going to give you advice on how to help your teens handle dating and sex in the next chapter, so for now I'm bringing the issue of "facials" up just to show you the potential pitfalls of what is on the Web. And since these sexual practices are now well-known, they seep into the background peer pressure, and so your child, whether or not he or she is actually using the Web to look at porn, is being affected by what's out there. This also means that whether or not you have software to filter the contents of what comes into your computer, those effects will still be felt by your child.

Of course porn existed before there were computers so it's not the porn per se that is the problem in my opinion, but it's the variety, the quantity, and the ease of availability that has multiplied the negative effects of porn. When porn was hard for a teenager to get, what was depicted in that erotica was considered as exotic. But when the images become commonplace, then what is depicted in those images becomes commonplace as well. And so what ends up happening is that sex, as depicted through porn, becomes the norm rather than sex as it has actually been taking place in bedrooms across America.

Ironically, in every other aspect of your life you've been setting examples for your children with regard to their behavior, but since your sex life is private—and should remain so—that ends up being the area where they are the most vulnerable to this sort of outside pressure. They don't know what's going on behind your bedroom door, so they can't emulate you as they do with practically everything else. When it comes to their own sex life, they're entirely on their own. The end result is that the effects of porn become more powerful because there are no counterbalancing real-life images with which to compare them.

So that leaves you as a parent having to not only try to block the entry of porn into your house, but also find a way of counterbalancing the effects that porn has on our society as a whole, and will have on your children as they discover what's out there for themselves. This means that to deal with the effects of porn is not as simple as merely putting software on your computer but also requires that you address the subject head on.

You're the Expert

To be effective, you have to seem as if you know something about sex, which goes back to what I said earlier in this book about not appearing to be asexual in front of your children. If you hug and kiss and hold hands in front of your children, then when you tell them how important love is to a sexual relationship, you're going to be more believable because you've been illustrating this for as long as they can remember. But if you try telling them about the importance of a loving relationship when as far as your children are concerned you and your spouse could be just two good friends who happen to share a bedroom (or worse, two enemies), then what you say won't be taken as seriously. You can order your child to empty the garbage because both you and the garbage are in your presence, but your words will have less of an impact on an activity that's done outside your presence, particularly if those words haven't been backed up by any action.

What to Say

So what should those words be? The bottom line of the message you want to communicate is that the material seen on screen, whether it be in the latest blockbuster, the number one hit on TV, a music video, porn, or the commercials made by Madison Avenue, is fictional, not real life. In the case of a science fiction movie, it's an easy argument to prove because extraterrestrials aren't roaming around to reinforce what is seen on screen. Your child may have seen all the Harry Potter movies, but she knows that she's not going to be admitted to Hogwarts. The closer what is depicted on screen is to real life, however, the more difficult it can be deflect the damage, especially when there are all these "reality" shows on TV these days, which further blur the distinction between reality and fiction. Of course what you see on these reality shows is not real, any more than a televised wrestling match is real, but for young people, the distinction can be harder to make than for an adult.

The problem with porn is that you do see two, or more, people actually engaging in sex. So to some degree it is "real." What's not real is the motivation—money rather than sexual desire—and the fact that the action is the result of the director's instructions and isn't voluntary. In other words, for these actors and actresses, it's a job. They're not having sex, they're working, no matter how big the smile on their face.

The one advantage of all this "reality" programming on regular TV is that it gives you the opening to start this discussion. I certainly understand that it's not going to be easy to just raise the issue that porn doesn't reflect reality out of the clear blue sky. Your teen is going to look at you as if you were crazy. But if you come upon your teen watching some "reality" show and during the commercial start a discussion about how unreal the show actually is, then I think you'll find it easier to segue into the subject of porn.

Body Image

While you're having this talk, there's another topic that you need to bring up: body image. Many young women today already have self-esteem issues when it comes to their looks because of all the superthin and bust-increased models and actresses that they see all over the place. And the women in porn films are cut from the same mold, for the most part. The epidemic of anorexia and bulimia is proof of the effect such women are having on teens. But it's young males who are most attracted to porn (though don't automatically believe that a daughter hasn't seen any porn), and what they don't realize is that the men in these films are also selected for their looks, in particular the size of their "equipment."

I am literally deluged with questions about penis size. It seems that every male whose penis doesn't measure up to those seen on screen feels like he's lacking and will be a complete failure with women, even though penis size is just not all that important to women. This may be an issue for fathers to deal with, but because of all the erotic images that are now available, one parent is going to have to tell his son not to compare his penis with those of porn stars. If a young man goes to bed with a woman assuming that there is a problem because of the size of his penis, then it becomes more likely that there will be a problem, though it will be psychological, not physical. Men need to have a certain amount of confidence in their equipment in order for it to work properly, and getting the message that size doesn't matter, especially supersize, has now become a topic that should be covered. (As a point of information you can tell your sons I also get questions from men with a very large penis or women who have a man with a large penis as a partner about the problems they have with sex, so that while a very large penis might look good on camera, it's not necessarily all that useful in the bedroom.)

But the main message that you should be giving when talking about porn is that sex is so much better when it's part of a loving relationship. The main problem with seeing this XXX-rated material is that it decouples sex from the relationship, and so young people, young men mostly, believe that having sex outside of the context of a relationship is not only all right, but something to be sought after. Sex becomes likened to a sport where each conquest is another victory, or notch on the bedpost. Obviously, this isn't a new idea as there have always been Casanovas and always will be. What is changing, however, is that this attitude is becoming more widespread so that it's not just a small percentage of young men who think this way, but many young men, whether or not they are successful at making the conquests they seek. For the unsuccessful, sometimes their lack of success is caused by this attitude. Because they're not looking for a relationship, because they're obviously only looking for sex, many young women are going to reject them. Here again is a case where I get a lot of questions from young men complaining that they're 15/18/21/25 and still a virgin because they can't find anybody to have sex with them. I always tell them to stop looking for a partner just to have sex with and start seeking out someone with whom they can fall in love. Not only will they be more successful, but the sex will be better too.

Of course there are young women, as young as 13 or 14, who do engage in casual sex. One or two young ladies among a group of guys can satisfy many of their desires. Often these girls do have low self-esteem, but I also believe that the atmosphere about sex has so greatly changed that it's not true of all of them. So you may have a daughter who appears to be well-adjusted but nevertheless is engaging in casual sex and who needs to hear from you.

These are not easy messages to give a child, though I believe it can be done in many cases without getting too deep into the nuts and bolts details. The key is to start soon enough so that your message gets through in time to inoculate your son or daughter somewhat before all the other messages about such concepts as "friends with benefits" reach them. As I said, I get into actual dating in the next chapter, but some of the messages clearly overlap, and in the case of erotica, the influence of one over the other is undeniable, as I've just been illustrating. Young people are impressionable. So much about them, from their bones to their personalities, have not yet been fully formed. As a parent you spend a lot of time with them and so have daily opportunities to make an impression, but I'll be the first to admit that it takes effort, it takes putting aside some of your own prudery, and it's not easy. You have to be ready to face the fact that your message may not be accepted, at least not openly. But I'm telling you that some, if not all, of your message will have a positive effect and so you must give it.

Q. In order to liven up our sex life, my husband and I sometimes look at an erotic DVD. We have about a dozen of them and we keep them in my husband's closet. Well, my 15-year-old son somehow found the stash. We know this because he left one in the DVD player. Since he knows we've been watching them, what do we tell him?

A. I guess I should begin by chastising you for not putting this material under lock and key. If you're not very careful about where and how you store such material, and that would include sex toys and other such items, you can be sure that a teenage child is going to discover them.

The one outcome you don't want to have happen as a result of this is that he decides that anything you've said about looking at sex on the computer is hypocritical and he has free rein to roam through all the Web sex sites. To avoid that, I'm going to suggest that you discuss what happened, acknowledge that he has sexual needs and masturbates, and offer him a replacement for your DVDs. What I would suggest is that it be copies of *Playboy*, that either come as a subscription or that his dad buy for him on the newsstand. Though I know the Hefners, both Hugh and his daughter who runs the company, Christie, I don't have any stock in their company and so the reason I bring this publication up from time to time in this book is because compared to what else is out there, *Playboy* is actually on the wholesome side. Your son will find the pictures sufficiently stimulating to aid in masturbation but you can take some comfort in knowing that he won't find anything in the magazine that's too outrageous. There is a problem that he will think that big-breasted women are the ideal, but since that image is everywhere—in movies, in magazines, on TV—seeing *Playboy* will not have that large an influence in this respect. (I have more to say on the subject of replacement porn later in this chapter.) You could also do nothing and pretend that it never happened, but that would only work if you were entirely comfortable with the material on these DVDs and felt really uncomfortable talking to your son about this because it involved your own viewing habits.

Let me add here that a couple like this could speak to their son and if he brought up their viewing habits just say to him, "That's a private matter and doesn't belong as part of the discussion." The problem with that is that while you may not want to discuss it, it will remain the gorilla in the room, as they say. He's going to pull some message from the fact that his parents watch porn, and so it would be better if it came with an explanation. You don't have to go into great detail, but a simple explanation that the two of you are a loving, married couple; and used within the confines of a relationship, an erotic DVD doesn't pose the dangers that it does to a teenager. I'm not saying that this will be a simple or easy discussion—far from it. It is going to be one that you're going to feel very nervous about; but on the other hand, it will provide you an excellent opportunity to have a heart-to-heart talk about some important subjects. You might feel that it would have been better had the DVD been put back, but in the end it may be a good thing that you got pushed into such a conversation.

By the way, I hope that any set of parents who get caught with such material will not delay in getting a lock for the closet door in which they store their erotica. Getting caught this way once is understandable, but not twice.

Blocking the Negative Effect

I think we're all on the same page now when it comes to the negative effectives of erotica on the Web, and I believe that you want to do all you can to limit your teen's access to the excesses available with this type of material. Your first line of defense is what you say to your children about this material and the harm it can do, though as you know, fear doesn't work over the long run so don't overdo it with your warnings. As I said earlier, filtering what comes into a computer will block some sites that have good information, so that's one reason to avoid having to censor what your teens can see. Blocking access to many sites also sends a message to your teens that you don't trust them. Since teens are by nature rebellious, that message may lead them to become more curious and go behind your back to seek out the sites they aren't supposed to be looking at in some other way, such as at a library or friend's house. So it's not clear-cut that you should definitely use blocking software where teens are concerned. But knowing that kids don't always obey your every command, as well as the strong lure that sexual material can have on young people whose hormones are raging, it most certainly is an option that you should consider, especially if some or all of the children at home are young.

Software

There exists various software designed to protect children by attempting to make sure that no sexual material can be downloaded into your computer, or at least any computer your kids are allowed to use, something that has to be said since so many homes have more than one computer with Web access these days. As I've said before, in doing this they may block sites that you wouldn't mind your son or daughter seeing, and they are also not 100% effective at blocking objectionable sites. But they definitely offer protection; especially if your children are at home for long hours without parental supervision, then such software might give you some added peace of mind.

There are a number of commercial packages including Net Nanny, CYBERsitter, CyberPatrol, MaxProtect, FilterPac, Netmap, Safe Eyes, WiseChoice.net, Cyber Sentinel, MSN Spy Monitor, and McAfee Parental Controls. They range in price from about $30 to $60.

There are also free filtering programs. The Family Online Safety Network (www.fosi.org) has a free filtering service which relies on sites to fill out a questionnaire listing anything that might be objectionable, like nudity or violence. This organization has the backing of many major corporations involved in the Internet including Microsoft, Verizon, and Cisco Systems. Other free filters include Parental Control Bar, K9 Web Protector, Crawler Parental Control, and Parental Filter.

I've only listed a few names here of both the free and for pay types of software. By the time you read this book, the list will probably have changed. My advice would be to do your own research on the Internet so you can get the most up to date information on these filters. It's also good to read reviews because that way you can see what other people have said, and their advice can be helpful as it's based on real-life situations and how well it worked with their children.

Of course the filter itself needs to be backed up by the speeches I mentioned earlier. Your children have to understand why you've put a filter on the computer. They have to understand that you know what's to be found out there, and your daughter especially has to know that there are strangers lurking who want to hurt her. If you can extract a promise from your children not to look at forbidden sites, then you can agree that the filter is there only to protect them from accidental exposure. But if you're at war over the use of filters, then it will become a battle of wills, with your teen doing everything possible to get over, under, or around the filter, and in the end I'd bet on your teen being successful.

Q. I bought some software to put on my computer that would prevent my two boys, ages 13 and 15, from going onto sex sites. They found out about it before I had a chance to load the software and they objected strongly. They said that I didn't trust them, and that if I didn't trust them with regard to sex on the Internet, how could I trust them in any other way. They had a point, and so I've kept the software in the box, but I also know how strong a pull sexual material can have. What should I do?

A. I wonder why you bought this software? How responsible do you think your sons are? Have they given you cause to doubt their sincerity? Or were you just generally worried about the dangers and decided to go ahead and buy the software?

Some children really value the trust their parents put in them, while others feel that they should be able to do whatever they want and so will try any trick to get around their parents' rules and regulations. Every parent has to make that decision, of whether their child is trustworthy or not. If you trust your boys, then don't install the software, but do keep an eye out. Check the computer's "history" which will tell you which sites they've visited. And if the history has been wiped clean, then you would have to assume that one of them had visited a site that he didn't want you to find out about. Then, you'll have to install the software.

Some parents might be wondering why I didn't just tell this mother to simply install the software and not take what the boys had said into consideration. The issue of trust is an important one. To some extent you can "bank" trust, so that in the future, when it is especially important—such as in the issue of drinking and driving, which could be lifesaving—you'll be relieved to know that you can trust your children. If you always assume that you can't, then there's a very good chance that you won't be able to. They'll always be looking for ways to break your rules if they think that you assume that they are breaking them anyway. But if there is trust, then their conscience will make it more difficult for them to break your rules, even if they're sure you'll never know about it. And it's because you can't be there to guide them every step of the way as they grow older, that you want to establish as much trust as possible so that you can be like a guardian angel working on their conscience even when you can't be there to physically protect them.

Kids Don't Need a Computer

There's a giant loophole in this idea of protecting teens with computer filters because these days there are many other ways to access the Web. If they have a laptop computer and go to a WiFi hotspot, that might allow them to circumvent filtering software, especially if they're intent on doing so. Many mobile phones these days have the capacity to download material from the Web. Even certain video game systems can offer Web access, like Nintendo's Wii, which has Web browsing capability, and Sony's PSP portable game player, which allows chatting with other players via a Bluetooth connection. Kids can also download videos into their iPods, and the porn industry didn't waste any time coming up with material for this potential audience: The selection of porn films to be played on DVD players, which most new computers can play, is in the tens of thousands.

So if you're locked into an all out battle with your teen, you may be able to limit his or her full access to the Web, but you're probably not going to be able to completely stop a teen from seeing material you find objectionable or from chatting with strangers. In the end, it's your relationship that matters most; it's the respect your teens have for your values and the love they have for you that will do the most to keep them safe. This is a process that began when they were born and must be backed up every day. In the long run, the communication you have with your children is the best weapon in keeping their communications with the outside world as safe as possible.

What if you discover that your teen has been acting inappropriately on the Internet? Hopefully, you'd already established some ground rules. If your teen knew that getting caught downloading porn or chatting with strangers was forbidden, then the punishment should already have been decided upon, which would probably include being cut off from using the computer. I say probably, because I know that in order to do their schoolwork, computer use may be required. But the computer and access to the Web can be two different things. Writing a report may only require using a word processor. If some research has to be done, the culprit is just going to have to wait until a parent gets home so that he or she can be supervised. How do you enforce such a rule? You could simply unplug the modem and take it with you or put it under lock and key. Then the computer would function but wouldn't be able to access the Web. Or you could install filtering software or software like the SnoopStick I already mentioned that will actually record the keystrokes used on the computer. Let the teen know that this software is permitting you to play sheriff and that should have the effect you're seeking, unless, of course he goes elsewhere for his fix of banned Web searching.

Replacement Porn and Erotica

Though as a parent you might not want to think about your teenager masturbating, we all know that most young males, and a lot of females, do masturbate. Assuming you're not ready to force them into an arranged marriage so that they can get sexually satisfied within the bounds of marital bliss, and also assuming that you prefer them masturbating to having sex with other teens with raging hormones, the question arises: If you've cut off their main source of material for sexual arousal, should you replace it?

Of course teens have been masturbating for eternity without the benefit of Web porn or cybersex, and so left to their own devices, most teens will still find ways to stimulate themselves to orgasm. But because they know about what is out there on the Web for free, the lure will still be there. This is one of those genies that is hard to put back in the bottle. Parents of teens 20 years ago didn't have these worries. In fact, they could probably not think about what their teens were doing behind closed doors because there wasn't much harm in what they were doing, nor were there any outside risks. (I know there may be some people whose religion forbids masturbation who won't agree with this, but apart from a religious prohibition, we should all be able to agree that masturbation is a safe sexual outlet.) So the question is, if there is a strong lure toward searching the Web for porn—and this applies mostly to teenage boys—and you don't want them to be engaging in such activity because of the nature of what they might find, would it be appropriate to get them a subscription to a magazine like *Playboy*, the content of which is quite mild compared to what is on the Web?

Every family is going to have to make their own decision on this topic, but I want to put it out there because I suspect that few sets of parents have actually even discussed this among themselves, no less gone ahead with such a plan. But that's probably not from a conscious decision but rather from the urge, when it comes to the sexuality of their children, for most parents to put their heads in the sand and pretend that their teens don't have the very same sex drive that their parents do. Of course that's nonsense, but nevertheless, it's a prevalent attitude. But whatever decision you as parents reach, I do hope that you'll at least talk about this option.

I also have another alternative, assuming that you don't want to get involved in the distribution of erotic images to your children, and that's to purchase some erotic books. *Lady Chatterley's Lover* is most certainly very erotic, though it's also well written. Some other classic erotica includes *Fanny Hill* by John Cleland, *Delta of Venus* by Anais Nin, and *Tropic of Cancer* and *Tropic of Capricorn* by Henry Miller. And if you read any of Nancy Friday's collections of sexual fantasies, such as *My Secret Garden* or *Women on Top*, I'm sure you'll find them arousing. By having some books like that on the shelf— don't worry, your teens will find them if you do—they'll be exposed to erotic content which might help them to masturbate, but you'll also be exposing them to some good literature. In fact, you might even find it enjoyable to read these books yourself. Whether or not to offer replacement erotica is a question that each set of parents is going to have to answer for themselves. For one thing, if your teen has younger siblings, you might not want such material lying around the house. So I'm not saying that supplying a teen with erotica is something you should do, but I do want to present it as an option.

Basically what I'm saying is, trying to push your teen's sexual needs under the rug may produce the opposite effect of what you want, which is why you actually need to consider their needs when putting together a framework of how to deal with sex on the Internet and in life in general. I'm not saying that this means that you should go sign up for that subscription to *Playboy*, but at the very least you need to give your teen some room to release his sexual urges. If you suspect that a teen is spending time in the bathroom masturbating, don't scream at him for it, unless you really need to use the bathroom. Instead, be glad that his sexual equipment works and that he's masturbating in your bathroom and not having casual sex somewhere else.

The Dreaded Return from College

When older teens come home from college on vacation, there is often some static between parents and students on several levels, including when to go to bed, curfews, drinking, and sex. In college there were no filters on their computers. In addition, word circulated quickly about which site had the hottest pictures. If you have younger children, then the issue of removing the filter won't be on the table as your college-aged child won't even ask. But what if there is no one at home too young to be offended but you've never removed the filter? Or else you had, but you're thinking of putting it back on? In my opinion, it's time to let go with regard to this issue. If you can't control your child for 9 months out of the year, trying to reestablish complete control for the other 3 months is going to cause needless friction. You have a perfect right not to allow a college student to bring back a boyfriend or girlfriend and expect this person to sleep in the same room. That's different. Even if they are having sex on campus, that doesn't give them the right to do it in your home. But to try to limit what they do on the computer, as long as they don't look at porn sites in front of you, is an issue I think you should leave alone.

For Girls

Let's say that at some point, some man disguised as a teen is able to develop an online relationship with your daughter, but then he lets her know that he's really a lot older. While you might expect that she would react negatively, she might not. She might take it as a compliment that an older man is interested in her. For that reason, you have to let her know, in no uncertain terms, that she cannot associate with older men, whether or not she meets them on the Web or anyplace else. This has to be an order, but also you have to explain to her the dangers.

I know that there are so-called May-December romances that work out just fine, but if that happens to her when she's an adult and supposedly understands the pluses and minuses, that's one thing. But an older man interested in a teenage girl is a sexual predator, period. She has to understand that fact so that she won't fall prey to whatever such a man might say to her to convince her that he's anything but a predator. There have been too many cases where young girls have fallen prey to these men for you to leave any loopholes.

For Boys

The definition of *addiction* requires that it be physical, such as to a drug, but psychological "addictions" do certainly exist, and an addiction to porn is one that I hear about all the time. A teenage boy who uses the computer to look at porn regularly could certainly develop such an addiction, which would be very hard to break as he got older.

Since looking at porn is an activity that your son is unlikely to tell you about, you can't wait until you possibly might discover . that he's looking at it to speak up. Again, fear alone won't stop someone from doing a particular negative activity, but letting him know about the dangers of an addiction to porn may at least get him to limit himself. This is not an easy subject to talk about with your teen, but it is an important one. Be on the lookout for any articles on the subject, and use such an article as an excuse to talk about this particular danger with your son.

CHAPTER 7

When Your Teen Starts Dating

N EW PARENTS EAGERLY await every one of their baby's "firsts": first smile, first time he rolls over, her first steps, and so on. Those good feelings at witnessing the child's progress continue as the baby grows up and goes through various phases— until the baby becomes a teen and the "firsts" have to do with sex. Developing an interest in the opposite sex, or the same sex, is a stage that every human goes through, and of course parents are happy that their children have the sexual desires they're supposed to have, but let's face it, this stage also comes with a lot of trepidation. When it comes to cutting the apron strings, dating is a major snip.

Let's start by analyzing why this is so. Some of it may have to do with your own dating experiences. If you had a few broken hearts or other problems during your dating years, that's naturally going to make you worry as your offspring enters the world of dating. And then there were the good parts: the kisses, the romance, the sex. For you, they were good, but for your baby? What it means is that your baby is not your baby any more, and so that's another reason for feeling nervous. And then there can be serious ramifications of dating and sex. What if you hate the young lady your son is dating? What if your daughter's dating a drug dealer? Or her beau has no manners? Sending your child off into the unknown is a scary proposition.

Sticking with the Pack

The best way for young teens to get into dating is to go in groups. There's much less pressure all around, especially for you. And you should actively encourage them to avoid pairing up as long as possible. But in the end it's out of your hands, and at some point your teen is going to have a girlfriend or boyfriend. And while that will scare you a little, it will also be a relief, because parents don't' want to see their child feeling left out. If most of your teen's friends are also without a steady date, then it's fine; but if they all start to form couples, then having your child be the odd man or woman out will also cause you concern.

You might think that you have no impact on how your teens and their friends interact, but that's not totally true. If you can find ways of facilitating their group get-togethers, that will encourage them to stick together. So if they need a ride to the movies, try to make yourself available. Stock up on snacks so that if they want to hang out in your basement, they feel welcome. If they seem bored, as teens often do, take out some old board games and put them where they can see them. Don't suggest that they play or they'll never go near them, but if they're around, you never know. Make an effort to get to know all of them. Your own teens may cringe at your attempts to speak to their friends, but if you're not a stranger, the bonds you create will actually help your teens: If their friends feel comfortable in your home, then they'll be more likely to come around; and when they're all at your house, at least you know what they're up to, which is always a relief.

You're going to have to learn to be a bit tolerant. A group of teens make noise and will usually leave a mess behind. If you come down too hard on your teens, then they're not going to volunteer your home as much. And if the group is elsewhere, you have no control over the situation whatsoever. No matter how raucous they're being, don't just go hide in your bedroom. If the group knows that you're hiding from them, you won't have much influence on their behavior. You want to make your presence felt so that no one will decide to light up a joint or raid the liquor cabinet.

A Lack of Friends

If your teen doesn't seem to have friends, then that is a problem. Because everyone needs to have friends, it makes your teen vulnerable. If the wrong person comes around, who may be seeking to use your teen rather than really be friends, your teen will never see it coming because she'll be so glad to have a friend. So you have to get to the bottom of why a child's social life is way below par. If you can't figure it out on your own, then send your child for counseling.

Benefits of Counseling

I understand why people hesitate to send a child for counseling. As a society, we look down on people who have a "mental illness," which can include depression, for instance. Rather than risk labeling your child, the temptation is that "she'll grow out of it." But psychological issues are just like physical ones in that the later you deal with them, the worse they get and the harder they are to fix. So despite the temptation to hope that the problem is just a passing phase, I strongly suggest that you take action and get professional help if you notice something peculiar in your teen's behavior. If you're not sure, then take your teen to see your family doctor. And if your teen brushes off the problem and tells you to mind your own business, don't listen. If you see signs of trouble, do whatever it takes to get to the source and deal with it.

There are also things you can do yourself. Try to see if you can figure out how to make your teen more appealing. Maybe if your basement had one of those wide-screen TVs, that might act as a lure. Or if your teen had the latest video games hooked up to it. If your teen is overweight and you think that is part of the problem, make a concerted effort to help cut some of those pounds by not buying junk food, signing her up for an exercise class, getting him a bike, or whatever else would be helpful.

While most teens make friends either at school or in the neighborhood, that's not necessarily the right approach for every teen. If a teen has a particular interest that is not shared by others, he won't fit in and also won't make the effort to do so. But such a teen still needs companionship. In cases like that, see if you can help your teen find others who like the same thing. For example, if your daughter loves to act but didn't make the school drama club or the school doesn't have one, find out if there's a drama group in town, and help her join. If your son likes to cook but his schoolmates think this is too weird, see if you can set him up with some sort of internship at a local restaurant. Even if the people there aren't his age, they'll share the same interest; and if he's serious, it could be a first step toward a career as a chef. Not every kid fits the general mold, and as your kid's parent, it's up to you to see where in society your child might fit best and then give him or her a boost to get there. Some teens are very resourceful, while others aren't, but once you get them headed in the right direction, they'll soar.

Dating

Eventually, most parents of a teenager will be having to deal with serious dating. And that is going to require another "talk" because no matter how thorough you were the first few times, at this juncture you have to make sure that you dot all your i's and cross your t's.

One of the biggest fears parents have with regard to talking about sex is that mentioning birth control and condoms for safer sex implies that they are giving their child the green light to actually engage in sex, so long as the child follows the rules about remaining safe. If the talk is given before the teen has started to date, then the time it will take to find a partner becomes a reassuring buffer zone that allows parents to let the word *condom* come out of his mouth. But when a teen is already dating, it means that the opportunity for actually having sex is close at hand, so I know that uttering statements about safer sex can cause panic to set in. But trust me, if you really want to feel panic, all you need to do is hear your child use the word *pregnant*. So this is a case of that noted ounce of prevention.

If your child is still a virgin, then I can guarantee you that the thought of having intercourse is even more scary to him or her than it is to you, and just because you speak about such matters isn't going to push any teen over the edge. If your child is not a virgin, then it's definitely worthwhile repeating the safe sex messages. So put aside your fears of causing your teen to have sex by talking about it. It's much more likely that the opposite will happen. If a teen is hesitating about having sex, being reminded of everything that can go wrong—like a condom falling off—will probably delay matters even more. I've said that scare tactics don't work, and they don't in the long run, but they certainly can in the short run.

There are other reasons for a teen to delay having sex besides just the dangers. Being in a serious relationship changes your life in many ways. In can certainly affect your studies. It may give you less time to be with your friends. It ties you down so that maybe you want to watch football but your girlfriend wants to go to the mall. If your teen is not already madly in love, in which case your words would fall on deaf ears, let your teen know that being in love has responsibilities. Since teens seem to prefer shirking responsibilities to grabbing them, this line of argument may have some success—not in stopping a teen from dating, but in keeping the relationship from getting too serious.

Friends with Benefits

Having said this, I know that for some teens these days that logic will have the wrong impact. They may say, "You're right, I'm not ready for a real relationship, but I do want to have sex, so I'm going to find some friends to have sex with." This is the concept from which the term *friends with benefits* is derived.

Obviously, I deplore such a concept. The main reason is that I believe sex should occur within a relationship. But another reason is that I don't believe that in such situations both people are actually just friends. My guess is that one party has feelings for the other, and rather than not spend time with that person, will use sex as a bribe. And I'm particularly afraid that this person will be a young girl being taken advantage of by a boy, particularly if she has any self-esteem issues.

In addition, a recent study of students at Michigan State University[§] showed that students in such a relationship are afraid to develop feelings for the other person in case those feelings aren't reciprocated. So here you have young people who might be able to fall in love but are holding back their emotions on purpose, and yet still having sex. To me there is nothing sadder. I'm a big believer in the pleasure that can be derived from sex, but I also know that such pleasure pales in comparison to the passion that exists when the two people are in love.

Furthermore, if someone is regularly releasing sexual tension by having sex with a friend, that person is going to be less inclined to make the effort to find a lover. So what such people are doing is wasting months and years of their lives when they could be sharing love with someone else.

Finally, what happens when someone who has been having sex with one or more friends does fall in love? Will his partner feel comfortable hanging out with his female friends with whom he's had sex or will she feel jealous? I think there's going to be a good chance she is going to feel jealous, whether openly or not, and so she's going to want to keep him away from these friends. And then if his male friends are friends with these females, this girlfriend (or boyfriend if the sexes are reversed) will be trying to keep them out of his life too. How complicated is that going to be?

I don't believe this friends with benefits concept is running rampant among teens. It's probably more likely to happen among 20-something-year-olds who are already sexually experienced. But once an idea like this gets out, then younger, impressionable people will pick up on it, particularly if it is depicted in popular TV shows and movies. So what should parents do with regard to this type of behavior? You have to be very frank and make sure that your teen knows that you are dead set against it and why. It should not be part of a message that says they should not have sex at all. If you offer them a blanket rejection of any sexual activity, then if they're going to disobey you for the least offense, it frees them to disobey you for every offense. The next thing you know, they're going to have their own set of friends with benefits, if not for inter-

§ Cary, B. (2007, Oct. 2). Friends with benefits, and stress too. *The New York Times.* From http://www.nytimes.com/2007/10/02/health/02sex.html

course, then maybe for oral sex. So you have to maintain a consistent message, and to me it's that casual sex is not only forbidden, but that it's not good sex, and even if you're in a relationship, sex is something that you have to be very sure about because it does come with a lot of responsibility.

Everybody's Doing It

Children of all ages are always using the excuse that "everybody's doing it." When kids are young, you can ignore them because you have more control and can enforce your rules. But it's much more difficult to do that with teens. And if all your daughter's friends who have boyfriends are telling each other about how they're having oral sex, the day she gets a boyfriend the pressure will be on for her to follow suit, not only from her boyfriend, but from her girlfriends.

I'm not going to promise that you can overcome this pressure, but you have to try, and the approach that I would suggest is to tell her that she's special. Now this is going to take more than words. You're going to have to go the extra mile to make her feel special. Don't go overboard, but do make a special effort. On Saturday morning, take her with you to have her nails done. If you see a nice top in a window, buy it for her, telling her she's special. If she wants to borrow a piece of your jewelry, tell her that you'll let her because she's special.

Telling her she's special is planting a seed. Through your actions, you'll be adding fertilizer to the idea. If you do a good job, hopefully the concept will become deep-rooted. Then if she's not sure about whether she wants to have oral sex with her boyfriend, she'll say no because deep down she'll be saying to herself, "I'm special and I'm not going to have sex with just anyone." There's no guarantee this will work, but it has the potential to have the desired results, and so my advice is to give it a try.

Of course if she does have the desire, then she probably will go ahead. But maybe that means that the relationship is a good one; and while it may bother you, it's not the end of the world. Your job, as I see it, is to get her to wait until she's really ready. Once she reaches that point, then it's ultimately out of your control.

Using the Media to Your Advantage

On the one hand, the media is always depicting sex as if there are no consequences and as if everyone is doing it, so that the young people who aren't are made to feel bad. But there is another side to this. Sadly, many of the media stars do suffer the consequences of their actions and they're always in the papers getting arrested or going in for rehab, or other such things. So from your point of view, as a parent, here are examples to hold up to your teens to show that "the good life" isn't all that good. Here are people with tons of money and fame, and they're not happy. They can't find satisfaction. They're hooked on the fast life, not just drugs or alcohol, even though it doesn't bring them any joy. And you can be sure your teens have seen these stories. What they perhaps haven't done is internalize them. They haven't made the connection between their lives and the lives of these celebrities. They may not fully understand that if they don't toe the line, they might end up going down the same dead-end street. So that's where you come in, but gently. Don't beat them over the head with the latest antics of this star or that singer. Instead discuss the incident with them and let them know how sad it is, how these people are wasting their talents and their lives. Make them appear pathetic, not evil. There's a certain appeal to evil, but there's no appeal to being pathetic.

The Prom

Whether your teen has a steady or not yet, there's one day of the year when every teen who's a senior, and often a junior, needs to have a date, and that's the night of the prom.

It's tempting to climb on my soapbox here and denounce the craziness that prom night has become, especially with relation to the cost, but I won't. The excessiveness that is my concern in this book has to do with sex. There are two phenomena that occur on prom night. The first involves those couples who are going steady. For some reason, lots of girls who've resisted going all the way feel that the time to give up their virginity is on the night of their senior prom. I guess some of the "pressure" comes from the fact that the prom signals that high school is just about over, and so to mark this new stage in life there's some need to lose one's virginity. But there's another reason that this occurs, and that's because parents have been coerced into allowing teens going to a prom to stay out all night without adult supervision. While the whole class is supposed to be partying together somewhere, the opportunity for couples to separate themselves and find a place to have sex is there for the taking.

Honestly, if two 17-year-olds who have been going out for quite a while and are in a serious relationship have sex, it's not the end of the world. However, if it's something that you're 100% against, then it's up to you to "ruin" prom night by making sure that your teen heads home when the official activities end. I just don't want to be there when you make this announcement.

I am much more concerned by the casual sex that also seems to take place these days on prom night. While a couple who have been planning on having sex on prom night for months will come prepared with a condom, or at least I hope they will, two people who are not part of a long-term relationship might not. Of course in these times they might be having oral sex instead of intercourse, but you never know. So this type of casual sex is very risky. Certainly no one is going to bother to find out if the other person has been tested for STDs.

An even bigger cause of concern is that whatever takes place might be because of alcohol or drugs. Alcohol is certainly not on the agenda at the prom, but in many cases teens find ways of circumventing such bans. I'm not even sure if it wouldn't be better if the prom-nighters could go to a bar and drink in a civilized manner rather than guzzle whatever liquor they can get their hands on in their cars or in an alley. Yes, it's possible to get quite drunk in a bar, but if the drinking takes place over a longer period of time, as everyone gets tired, the pace of drinking may slow down. However, if the idea is to get as drunk as possible in the shortest amount of time, then the effects are going to be multiplied. And drunk teenagers are not going to be responsible when it comes to sex.

Finally there's the danger of date rape. If a young lady is just about out cold, she may wake up to find that she's no longer a virgin, and it's also possible that she may not know who took her virginity, and whether anyone else participated. Alcohol is not the only danger; there are drugs that someone can put into a drink that the victim will not be able to taste or sense in any way, but soon enough that person will be powerless to stop herself from being raped, nor will she remember what happened either. I'm not saying that these drugs are that easy for a high school senior to get, and that such rapes are commonplace, but they certainly do occur, though mostly as a result of alcohol rather than date rape drugs.

Prom night used to be fairly civilized, but teens have been pushing the envelope for a long time so that now for many high schoolers it's got the quality of a bacchanal. That's sad, but I guess it's one more genie that we can't put back in the bottle. If it's a junior prom, you as parents should be a lot more conservative. Seniors are on the verge of breaking away, so you don't have as much control. But at the very least, you should give your teen the "be careful" speech one more time.

When You Know Your Teen is Sexually Active

Some teens couple up and become two peas in a pod. You may want to pretend that they're not having sex, but burying your head in the sand is not a good tactic. I'm definitely against your allowing them to sleep together overnight in one of your bedrooms. You don't have to be a doormat. But you're not going to be able to watch them every minute of the day and night, and so you have to face the reality that you're not going to be able to put an end to their sex life. And once you've faced that fact, you then have to decide whether you want to become grandparents while your teen is just that, a teen.

If used properly, condoms are relatively safe with regard to protecting from an unintended pregnancy, but they're not as safe as the pill. So if you have a daughter who` you are fairly sure is sexually active, then you might want to offer her a visit to the gynecologist to go on the pill. Now she might turn you down because while she and her boyfriend may be engaging in sexual behavior, they haven't graduated to intercourse yet. In that situation, there is a small risk that because you held up the possibility of her going on the pill that she'll see that as a green light to have intercourse.

But I do believe it is a small risk. In the first place, if she's held back up to this point, she has many reasons for doing so, not just because she was afraid of what you would think. And in your speech, you're going to reinforce those reasons. Remember, you're not giving her the green light, but instead reminding her of the serious consequences that sex can have. But you're also treating her as an adult, so that instead of having sex out of rebellion, she'll only do it when she's ready. And if you've raised a sensible girl, if she's sure that she's ready, then she probably is.

Some parents decide not to leave anything to chance, and so they place condoms in a drawer in the house and say to their teens that if they're needed, to just use them, that no one will be keeping count. If you're pretty sure that your teen is sexually active, then that's not a bad idea. If something happens, you're going to pay a price in any case, in worries if nothing else, so rather than just ignore the reality of the situation, taking charge of providing contraception makes a lot of sense.

When is a Teen Ready?

Many people ask me at what age someone should start having sex, and I always have to tell them that there is no set age. When it comes to driving, voting, or drinking, your status does switch from one day to the next when you hit that milestone birthday, but those are artificial restrictions. When it comes to having the maturity to enter a sexual relationship, for some, though admittedly few, 14 is the right age, while there are others who've reached their 21st birthday and are still not mature enough or have not found the right partner, which is an important deciding factor, at least in my book.

You have to remember that throughout most of mankind's history, it was common for young people to get married in their early to midteens. If our children don't have the maturity at that age, it's not because they're not physically ready but rather because we've held them back emotionally. We, as a society, have decided to treat teens as not yet having reached adulthood because we want them to stay in school and they require parental support to do so. But just because we've done everything possible to make sure that a

14-year-old is not an adult doesn't mean that some 14-year-olds haven't managed to reach adulthood despite our best efforts. They may not pick up their dirty clothes off the floor because they know that you'll do it for them, but if they were put in a responsible position, they'd be able to take care of themselves. And having sex, assuming you can prevent a pregnancy, is the least important of the many adult responsibilities. In many, many countries, 14-year-olds do hold down full-time jobs and do support families. So it's not that a 14-year-old is innately incapable of acting like an adult but rather that we force a lengthened childhood upon them. And therefore under these artificial conditions, clearly the vast majority of 14-year-olds are not ready to have sex. But some are, and many more reach that state as each year passes.

If you have a pot of boiling water and try to push the top down further and further into the pot, you're going to have a harder and harder time, and if you let go for even a second that top is going to burst off because of the added pressure you've caused. It's the same with a teenager. The more pressure you exert, the greater the internal temperature of the teen, and at some point there can be an explosion, or in the case of some teens, that can be a daily occurrence. But you have to understand that you are creating this artificial pressurized situation. You're intentionally keeping them from becoming a full-fledged adult. Given the needs of a long education in our modern society, I'm not saying that you're necessarily wrong. All I'm trying to get you to do is acknowledge that your teen is not a child and so the conflict over many issues, including sex, is one to be navigated. There is no one answer that will fit every teen. Some teens couldn't hold down a job flipping hamburgers at McDonalds while others could manage a Fortune 500 company. Some teens are so ready to have sex that there's no stopping them, while others don't really mind not having the responsibility of having a steady boyfriend or girlfriend. So you have to adjust your parenting to fit your teen, and you may not always be happy with the outcome. For example, being in a steady relationship is likely to have a negative effect on a teen's grades in school simply because being in a relationship takes a lot of time, which takes away from the time to study. But if a teen has formed a relationship, there's nothing you can do to change that, and if you did manage to keep them apart, your teen's grades would probably worsen rather than get better. So you have to learn to adapt to the realities of your teen. You can guide teens, but only so far. If you're constantly butting heads, then you have to look carefully at the overall situation and try to figure out how to reduce the pressure so that there are fewer explosions. You have to recognize that you are not in full control, that your teen is slowly breaking free, and you have to choose your battles carefully. Sometimes sex is an appropriate battleground and sometimes it's not. And if it appears that you're not going to be able to enforce celibacy on your teen, then you have to do whatever is necessary so that at least your teen is having sex as safely as possible, which may mean making that appointment with the gynecologist to get your daughter a prescription for the pill.

Parents of sons have a slightly easier time because it is not their child who can get pregnant. But your teen can certainly cause a pregnancy, and so you can't be left off the hook. You have to talk to your son to make certain that he's being careful. Exactly what you say may depend on your son. If he's generally responsible, then you don't have to be as repetitive about your warnings as if he's a daredevil.

As I said in the chapter on peer pressure, if your teen wants to be treated more like an adult because he or she is in a serious relationship, now is the time to give your teen more responsibility, not less. When a teen gets a drivers license, you might sit her down and say, "In exchange for using the family car, I'm going to ask you to drive around your younger siblings from time to time, and get a part-time job to pay for gas." In this situation you might say, "If you're old enough to be in a serious relationship, then twice a week I expect you to prepare dinner or do the family shopping." What the responsibility will be will depend on many factors, such as which responsibilities the teen already has, but my point is that you want to underline the fact that with the perks of adulthood come the duties.

What effect might this have? Throughout history, the privilege of having sex was tied to marriage, which of course carried with it tons of responsibilities. When you decouple sex and responsibilities, young people look at it as a form of recreation and you get many of the problems we see, like the rampant spread of sexually transmitted diseases. So it's important to try to make that connection in their minds, that with adulthood come certain freedoms but also certain responsibilities.

It's important to set up the consequences ahead of time. I don't think it's enough to tell your teen that she's spending too much time with her boyfriend. Instead you have to say, "I think you're spending too much time with your boyfriend and it's probably going to affect your grades negatively; and if that happens, I'm going to set up much stricter limits." Then it's up to her. Either she maintains her grades or you'll force her to spend more time at home studying. Because she's going to have a strong motivation to keep those grades up, so that she can see her boyfriend, you might be pleasantly surprised. And by giving her plenty of notice—and by plenty I don't just mean in advance, but to repeat this warning often—if her grades go down, she'll probably limit how much she rebels when you clamp down. Of course, you can't be weak. You have to follow through with what you said you'd do, or otherwise you'll lose all control.

Studying is clearly the most important activity in which your teen could be engaging, but the problem is that neither one of you will see the results for quite some time, until the next report card period. So I think the conditions you set up have to be a mixture of both schoolwork and household chores. You can tell immediately if the dishwasher's been emptied, the garbage thrown out, the shopping done, or a sibling driven to piano lessons. And then if the goal isn't met, you can dole out a relatively mild restriction as far as dating is concerned. It may take a few nights spent at home for your teen to understand that you're serious, but eventually that message will sink in. And that type of immediate feedback, that shirking responsibilities means losing the privilege of dating for at least a short time, could go a long way toward getting her to work a little harder at her schoolwork.

I Hate Him/Her

What happens if you can't stand the person your teen is dating? The first thing you have to do is look at this young person objectively. Does he or she represent some danger to your child? Or is it just that this person gets on your nerves but isn't all that bad? If it's the latter, then there's not much you can do. Luckily, you don't have to spend that much time with this person, though sometimes that might not be true if the couple spend most of their time together at your house. (Which may not be such a bad thing since you get to supervise them when they're under your roof.) But the more serious situation is when the person your teen is dating clearly is not someone you want associated with your child.

What happens in many instances is that the parent tries to break the couple up, the teen resists, and then parent and child are at each other's throats. Even if the teen had some doubts about the relationship, rather than give in to parental authority, the teen is going to do everything possible to hold on to the relationship. So declaring war on your teen is just not a good tactic, both because it probably won't work and because it will close you off from your child, which could lead to other negative consequences. For example, if your son knows that you don't like the girl he's dating because you think she's not right for him, but you don't go overboard trying to get them apart, he might resist having sex with her to prove that the relationship is not based on something as lowly as just sex, but that he really loves and respects this girl. But if you try everything possible to split them up, then they'll cleave together, and it may be more likely that they'll end up having sex.

If you find yourself faced with such a situation, your first job, before you say a word, is to fully assess the situation. If you try to break the twosome up, there is going to be all-out war between you and your teen. I'm not saying that you may not want to assert all the authority you can muster in order to break up the couple, but don't do it without thinking through all the possible consequences because while you can't foretell the outcome, you do want to have an idea of what might happen. For example, what if because of the pressure you put on them, the couple decides to elope? Then you'd be worse off than if you hadn't done anything. But even without going to such extremes, if you become enemies with your child over this, you can end up losing control more than exercising control. So you have to tread carefully. For example, if you think your daughter's boyfriend is bad news, you could ask one of her best friends what she thinks about him. If he's really bad news, and if she's really a true friend, she'll tell you at least part of the truth. Maybe her assessment will be, "Yes, he has a lot of tattoos but he's really a nice kid" or else she'll tell you that he not only uses drugs, but sells them. By doing your homework, you'll have a better understanding of the situation and can then plan out the best course of action. But if you let your emotions take over, then the outcome is going to be less certain.

If you believe that your daughter has been brought up to know the difference between right and wrong, plus she is a bright and capable child, then in the end you have to have faith that your daughter is going to do the right thing. If you are attacking her, however, you're weakening her. If she's undergoing an internal battle between her conscience and her attraction for her boyfriend, and then she also is confronted with a battle against her parents, that might tip her toward making the wrong decision. If she's feeling overwhelmed, then it will be harder to be completely rational. I'm not saying that you shouldn't speak your piece. As a parent you have a duty to give advice to your child if you think she's making a mistake. Whatever her immediate reaction, she will take that advice back with her and think about it and use it to make her decisions. But if you step over the line and go from advice giver to authoritarian, then she may not weigh it carefully but could simply dismiss it because of its source, parents who are clearly "against" her. Remember, we may treat teens as children, but they are young adults, and part of the growing-up process is breaking away from the authority of their parents. It's better for all parties if this is a gradual process, but if you push her up against a wall, then it can happen all of a sudden. And if it seems more important at the time for her to assert herself in order not to be treated as a child, then she might make the wrong move, because instead of making a conscious decision, it will be an emotional lunge for freedom. So while it's okay to push, you have to understand that there is a limit so that you don't push her over the edge.

Getting Professional Help

If it appears that the choice is either giving in or all-out war, you should really consider seeking the assistance of a child psychologist. There are several reasons for this. First of all, taking your teen to see a professional is going to make quite an impression. It's

going to tell your teen loud and clear that you are seriously concerned about this relationship. Your son or daughter may also open
up to a professional in a manner that wouldn't take place with you.
Of course the psychologist will not tell you what your teen reveals,
but if a professional tells you there's not much to worry about,
then that will bring you some relief. And if your teen is in way
over his or her head, then the psychologist should prove helpful in
assisting your child to make the right choices.

Bringing in an Arbitrator

Your alternative to going to a professional is asking a close relative to step in. If your son respects your brother, for example, then
he may open up to him. Your brother won't have the authority to
tell him what to do, so your son may be more apt to listen to his
uncle's advice because it is not a command. And even if he doesn't
end up following it exactly, this advice may have a positive effect, if
not immediately, then in the long run. It will also serve as an outlet
for your son's emotions. When you talk to him, the situation might
quickly escalate into a screaming match, where not much communicating takes place. You're both likely to be on the defensive. But
someone a little outside the situation, like an uncle, will listen. He
won't have an agenda and your son will sense that. And by being
able to pour out his heart, assuming he can, your son will release a
lot of pent-up emotional energy. His uncle may get through to him
after that, and your son will be more likely to accept the advice. Of
course in the end his uncle may agree with your son. He may say
that your son should be allowed to date this girl, that there's really
nothing wrong with the relationship. Since that's a possibility, you
should only bring in a relative if you trust his or her judgment,
because in the end, you will have to listen to this person's advice.
I'm not saying that you have to heed every word, but if you call in
an arbitrator, it's always with the understanding that this objective
person could decide that the other side is right. But if you trust the
judgment of this other person, then I think you have a lot more to
gain than to lose. You may have to admit that your emotions have
clouded your vision with regard to this relationship, but backing

down in such a situation is a good thing, especially if it keeps a rift from growing between you and your child.

The Value of Patience

If this is your daughter's first serious boyfriend and you can't stand him but he doesn't pose an obvious risk to your child, such as being a drug dealer or drunken driver, you have to keep in mind that in all likelihood he is not going to be the man she marries. She's still a teenager and will probably have several boyfriends before she settles on one to marry, who will become your son-in-law. So while you may think that this current beau is a creep, by waiting it out, he may disappear without you having to take any action. In fact, if you are pressuring her to break up with him, she may continue to see him for a longer period than she would if you weren't actively prodding her to dump him. Teenagers do act against their own interests sometimes out of sheer rebellion. So the very best course of action may simply be patience. Even if the two of them are constantly in each other's company and it appears that they're headed for marital bliss, there's a good chance that the veil of blindness caused by love will drop one day soon and she'll give him the boot.

But She's Only Thirteen!

It's usually the older teens that couple up, but it certainly does happen to younger teens as well. While the age of your child does make a difference in your eyes, it won't in hers. If she's head over heels in love, she won't care how old she is, but you're not going to give her the freedom of an older teen either.

What I said about patience above applies doubly so with a younger teen. You can be certain that this crush is not going to last, so it would make no sense for you to go overboard, no matter what your feelings about this other person. (If a young teen's crush is much older, you may have to intervene more strongly.) What I would advise is to keep a younger teen who is in a relationship under as tight a leash as possible. In other words, don't try to keep them apart, but don't let them out of your sight either. There's a good chance that young teens will appreciate this surveillance, even if they complain bitterly. If your teen is not ready for a serious relationship, parental supervision will allow your teen to stay within limited boundaries. So rather than fight this relationship, just keep a sharp eye on it.

Latch-Key Teens

One problem faced by many families is that both parents work, and so their teen is in an empty house for several hours every day. The term *latch-key* doesn't usually apply to teens, but let's face it, they're even more likely to get into trouble than younger children. And that's particularly so if they have a "steady." If the two of them can spend hours together with complete privacy, that's going to increase the odds that they may go further than even they originally planned.

As I've said before, you can't really stop teens from engaging in sexual behavior because they're resourceful, and the urge to have sex is strong. But if you make it too easy for them, then they're more likely to wind up having premarital sex. But how can you supervise a teen when you're not around? The only way is to find some other sets of eyes. If there are grandparents living nearby, then they should have the authority to make surprise visits. If you've got a neighbor who is home and can see who goes in and out, then perhaps you can recruit them to help you. I mentioned the SnoopStick earlier. If you can check whether your teen is online or not, forgetting for the moment what he or she is doing online, then at least you can be sure that your teen isn't in bed with somebody else. Teens tend to be messy, so if you're careful to check for signs that more than one person was at home, you might discover incriminating evidence. Obviously, if there are other children at home, you can recruit their help. You might encourage your teen to get an after-school job so that he or she isn't at home that much alone.

If you proceed with any or all of the abovementioned ideas, it's likely that your teen is going to complain that "You don't trust me." Your response has to be that it's not about trust, but about protecting your teen from temptation. If given enough leeway, temptation will overcome your prohibitions about bringing a girl-friend or boyfriend into an empty house. So you have to explain that you're just trying to help your son or daughter to have the strength not to give in to temptation.

I understand that a 17-year-old high school senior is going to feel that you can't control him or her. To some degree they're right. But whatever they do on their own, they do not enjoy the right to break your rules in your home. That is one law that you are fully entitled to impose, and you don't have to apologize for it. So on some issues you can be somewhat flexible, and on others you re-ally have to draw the line. You don't want to do it in a way that is confusing to your teen, who will then choose to ignore rules that he or she doesn't like. Instead, you have to be very clear and make sure that they know there will be serious consequences if they don't obey, and don't back down if and when it comes time to enforce the rules.

For Girls

Girls mature faster than guys, and so quite often teenage girls entering high school are not as interested in their fellow fresh-men guys, but dream about the upperclassmen. The problem is that those guys who were once freshmen and now are upperclass-men also have their sights on the freshmen girls. They know that they're not as wise as the older girls and can be taken advantage of. A freshmen girl might be very happy basking in the attention she's getting from the upperclassmen, though she might not be quite so glad if she knew the reason behind it.

While I don't think a one-year age difference is that much of a problem, if a junior or a senior starts flirting with your freshman daughter, then I would definitely be concerned. She may love the attention, but then subsequently feel that she has to act as if she was older, sexually speaking, in order to keep it. On the other hand, his only desire may be to have sex with her, and those dynamics are not good ones. Your daughter is going to know that you're not going to approve of such a relationship and so will probably try to hide it from you. That's why you have to be very explicit before she goes through the high school doors for the first time about this danger. If she knows ahead of time that a senior trying to get her attention may only be in it for the sex, she'll be more cautious. This knowledge is no guarantee that she won't get swept off her feet, but if it's going to have any effect, it must be given ahead of time, not after the quarterback of the football team has given her his sweater.

For Boys

There are advantages and disadvantages at being the one who has to take the initiative when it comes to dating. The advantage is that you don't have to sit at home by the phone; the disadvantage is that you are sure to get rejected, at least once in a while. Some boys, after a number of rejections, just give up. They become gun shy, and if they do approach a girl without any confidence, then the odds of her saying yes are going to be quite small.

Just because your son may always have gone to school with girls, don't assume that he knows how to go about getting a girl to agree to go out on a date with him. While he may not want to admit that he's having problems in this area if you ask him about it, he won't be adverse to hearing some advice. Much of this book has been about telling your kids what not to do, but in this case, a few lessons on how to go about attracting the opposite sex wouldn't be a bad thing.

CHAPTER 8

If Your Child is Gay

THERE ARE VARIOUS statistics that say such and such a percentage of people are gay or lesbian. (There is some confusion with regard to the terminology of homosexuality. *Homosexual* refers to both men and women who are sexually attracted to people of their own sex. *Gay* can refer to only men or be substituted for homosexual, and that's how I will be using it. *Lesbian* is a term only applied to women.) I'm not one to put much faith in such statistics, but more important, from any individual's point of view, these statistics don't matter. If one of your children turns out to be gay, then that's all that counts. How many other families out there share in this phenomenon is not relevant to you. It's your child who is gay, and you're the ones who have to live with this fact.

We don't know for certain what makes people prefer their own sex to that of the opposite sex. (Or for that matter why some people are transgender or transsexual or any of the other variants.) We suspect that the cause is genetic, and I, for one, go along with that explanation. One reason is that I get kids as young as 9 and 10 reaching out to me wondering if they are homosexual and ardently wishing that they weren't. These children haven't chosen their lifestyle anymore than left-handed children have chosen to be left-handed. Whether or not their environment had a role to play, I don't know, but clearly for children to know at such a young age that they are homosexual proves to me that they have not chosen this lifestyle, and therefore can't later decide to change back.

Accepting this as fact is key for any parent of a gay child. If you continue to hope that maybe your gay child is going to one day give up this lifestyle, then you won't be able to fully accept him or her.

Since this hope is baseless, the best course of action is to force it out of your thoughts whenever it pops up. You and your homosexual child are going to have a long future together, and you have to look forward together rather than look backward in a vain attempt to see if there might have been something you could have done differently. There wasn't; so just accept that fact and move on.

Of course, don't jump to conclusions and assume you have a homosexual child just because he or she is different. Yes, many professional dancers are gay, but that doesn't mean that a young man who likes to dance is automatically gay. Your child will let you know what his sexuality is when the time is right. If you have any doubts, don't try to push your child in either direction. This is an issue your child is going to have to sort out for himself. All you can do is be on the lookout for any problems your child's sexuality might be causing and then see if you can help.

For example, one reason a teen might not have any friends is because of his or her sexuality. A gay teen can end up being ostracized, or else just doesn't want to be with others because he's tired of having to hide his true identity all the time. Therefore, if your child has no social life and you have other reasons to suspect that she's gay, you might want to have a talk. If she won't open up to you, then offer her the possibility of seeing a counselor of some sort.

A gay teen is going to feel even more lonely if he feels that he'd be rejected by you if you knew he was gay. He may realize that eventually he's going to meet other gay people who will accept him; but for a teenager, potentially losing the support of his parents would be devastating, and sadly that does happen to many gay teens. So if you notice that your son doesn't have a social life, and you suspect it may be because of his sexuality, then your job is to be extra supportive. Make sure that if he has nothing to do on a weekend night that at least you're there for him. Offer to take him to the movies or play a board game.

Q. My 14-year-old son has pretty much admitted that he is gay. I've talked to him about it, and he says maybe it's not 100%, but from what I can see, it is. I'm a bit upset but try not to show it, but his father gets furious if I even hint at the possibility. My son knows how his father feels, and I'm sure that is preventing him from fully accepting himself. How do I handle this situation?

A. This is a very complex issue because the interpersonal relationships of every family are different. One parent might be more open than the other, or the parents may be more accepting than the siblings. In my opinion, not only would your child benefit from some counseling, but so would you. Your son could at least open up to a counselor, and that might be a big relief. And the counselor should also be able to play a helpful role in getting your husband to accept the true nature of his son's sexuality.

I think the first step that parents of a gay or lesbian child should take is to contact Parents, Families, and Friends of Lesbians and Gays (PFLAG). This is an organization that may be very helpful to you. Through PFLAG you can talk to other people who've gone through the process, and it can be very comforting to know that you're not alone. Also people who have already gone through the process will be able to give you guidance and keep you from making mistakes that others have made. If there is a local chapter in your area, by joining you'll immediately have an instant support group. And even if there isn't, join the nearest one because these days with all the means of communication open to us, you'll still benefit even if you can't attend meetings and see people face to face.

Another way in which PFLAG members may be able to assist you is by steering you toward counselors who specialize in the field of helping people accept their sexual identity. Since your child will be establishing a very personal relationship with any counselor, and we therapists are a bit of a blind item for the most part, getting personal recommendations could be very important to getting the help you need. And by the way, PFLAG is not just for parents, it can also lend support to your child as well.

Finding that you have a gay child is not supposed to be easy. It's not just one of those phases that all parents go through like the "terrible twos." I don't want to make it seem like it's an awful experience. You're not losing your child, you are only going to have to adjust to different expectations. But if you overreact, then you could lose your child, and that's why if you need help in adjusting to this new reality, then make sure that you get it. If you were alone, that would be one thing, but since you're not the first family going through this, and there an organization and counselors that specialize in assisting families in your situation, make sure that you take advantage of this source of aid.

Discovering that your child is gay is one thing, but having him or her start dating is another whole step that you're going to have to face. As long as it was theoretical, you didn't really have to think about it that much. But once your gay son or daughter is going out with other gays, then that will change the dynamics. Even if you've gone through counseling and thought you had come to grips with this aspect of your child's life, you may need to return to the counselor when you come to this stage of your teen's life.

If you have a gay son, you're going to have to become extra vigilant when it comes to matters of sexually transmitted diseases. For whatever reason, after the first wave of AIDS hit the gay community, young gays are once again engaging in unsafe sex practices. That is a recipe for tragic consequences. To avoid such a situation is the reason that you must try to get your entire immediate family to accept your gay child and to maintain that support as he begins to date.

If a young person feels that he (or she) cannot bring a gay person home and announce that this is his partner, that is going to have an unfortunate effect. Rather than try as hard as possible to form a relationship with one individual, your teen's goal might become to merely satisfy his sexual urges. And that can easily lead to becoming a part of the scene at gay bars where people have anonymous sex, often unprotected. So your job as parents is to make sure that your son or daughter knows that you will put out the welcome mat for any person that he or she is dating. It's not always easy for gay people, especially gay men, to find a partner because of the gay bar scene. So any obstacle you put up may be just enough to make it impossible, psychologically that is, for your son to put in the extra effort it takes to find a partner. And since he won't quite fit in with other straight people, you can see the attraction of the gay scene where he will be fully accepted, but which also offers the perils of unsafe sex. So even if it is difficult—and I'm not saying it's going to be easy—you have to swallow whatever antigay feelings you've had and learn to fully accept your child. And because this is difficult, I must repeat that finding outside support can be critical to being able to accomplish this goal.

Easier Said Than Done

I recognize that it's a lot easier to give advice than to put someone else's advice into effect. Let's say that you've accepted your gay child but your spouse cannot. Now you find yourself between that rock and hard place, fighting with your spouse, putting your marriage at risk over the sexuality of your child, who eventually is going to grow up and move out. The answer is that sometimes you have to compromise, and sometimes you don't. If your spouse is showing a side that you never saw before, perhaps you take a stand and risk your marriage because maybe there are other parts of your marriage that aren't in the best condition because of that attitiude. On the other hand, if you really love your spouse and want to spend the rest of your days together, then you'll have to soften your stand and do the best you can for your child while keeping your marriage going.

Having a gay child in our society can be difficult (though compared to other problems your child could have, physical or mental ones, it's really not that bad). The strong stigma attached to being gay absolutely makes it difficult for families, even if they are completely accepting of their child's sexual identity. However, if everyone involved truly tries to adapt, eventually time should heal any wounds that arise from either the initial discovery or later reaction.

As for your gay teenager, exactly how rough this growing up period is going to be will depend on many factors. Sometimes having even one good friend in whom your teen can confide can be enough to help weather the many storms that will inevitably have to be faced. But some gay teens really suffer, and the rate of suicide for gay teens is much too high. As I've said before, you may not be able to handle all the pressures yourselves, and so you should definitely consider counseling, especially if your teen seems to be having problems. There is also a Web site I can recommend called The Trevor Project (www.thetrevorproject.org). It is based on a film about a 13-year-old gay boy who tries to commit suicide when he is rejected by his friends. The site offers a 24-hour crisis hot line and a Q&A section where questions will be answered anonymously, and they'll even send a kit that includes a copy of the film. But if you sense that your teen has reached a crisis point, don't hesitate to take him or her to the emergency room. Sometimes immediate action has to be taken and it's better to overreact in such cases than decide to act after it's too late.

Coming Out

At some point, most gay people *come out,* which is the shorthand way of saying they "come out of the closet," that is, they reveal that they are gay. In some cases this revelation is made to everyone and in others only to some people. But to whatever extent a gay person is willing to reveal his or her sexuality, the coming out process is usually a slow one.

The first person a gay teen must admit his homosexuality to is of course, himself. That's usually followed by one or two close friends. Eventually family members are let in on the secret. If you have a teen who you suspect is gay, you shouldn't force the issue but rather you have to allow your child to set the timing of such an announcement. What you can do, however, is try your hardest to let your teen know that you will accept this announcement. Whatever your opinion of gay people had been, hopefully you can be accepting now that your child is seemingly going to join this group. If you've made comments in the past in front of your child that were antigay, then you have to repair the damage by going out of your way to let your child know that you do understand that some people are gay and that you can accept it if one of them turns out to be a child of yours. This will be much easier if both parents are on the same page, but if that's not the case, then it's even more important that the parent who is supportive lets the teen know that he won't be rejected.

Once your teen has let you know, she's probably going to ask your help in letting other family members know. That may happen when she's still a teenager, or she may not be ready and will ask you to keep it a secret for a while longer. You should cooperate either way. If you start spreading the news before she's ready for it to be broadcast—and you can rest assured that news like this will travel fast among a family even if you only tell one or two people— then that could end up being very painful for her. It takes courage to make such an announcement and while you can never be fully prepared, your teen can be underprepared. Teens need their social network and she might be very worried that if her friends find out, they'll drop her like that proverbial hot potato. So while she might seek some comfort in telling you, she might also feel betrayed if you let the secret out too early. If a teen is not ready to face the world as a homosexual, let the issue rest. At some point, when the teen has reached full adulthood, she'll be better able to make this announcement. That's especially true if she has found a partner who can lend her moral support.

For Boys

While no parent has ever been happy to discover that their child was a homosexual, since AIDS hit the gay community as hard as it did, the worries of parents have only increased. Sadly, more and more young homosexuals are having sex in situations that are anything but safe. The gay bars and baths that had disappeared are now back.

Part of the reason is that too many young people have decided that they no longer have to be as careful because there are so-called cocktails of medicine that can keep the ravages of AIDS at bay. Your job as the parent of a gay male is going to have to be to convince your son otherwise. First of all, these cocktails are quite expensive. And while they may add years to the life of someone infected with HIV, for a young person, that is just not long enough. Your gay son may not want to hear the truth, but your job is to make sure he hears it.

For Girls

While any gay person feels pain when their family rejects them, it's a little harder for young women because in general they tend to stay closer to the nest. Men are supposed to break free, but a woman will often be very close to her mom. Obviously, that's not true for every daughter. My suggestion if you, as a parent, are having difficulties accepting your daughter's homosexuality, is to definitely go for counseling. It will not only help you, but it will also be very helpful to your daughter if you can keep those bonds with her as close as possible.

Conclusion

I
T'S TEMPTING to conclude by offering up the old platitude, that teens have always given their parents problems and they always end up surviving. Of course that's true, but we're not talking in generalities here, we're talking about your child. It's similar to when the Today Sponge came out. There was a risk of a woman who used it dying from toxic shock but the odds were only one in 100,000. I came out against this product because right away I thought, "What if that one is my daughter?"

So with respect to the multitude of dangers that we've covered in this book, you do have to take them seriously because if something were to happen to your child, the consequences might be quite scary. But having said that, as long as you do the best you can, then you can't allow yourself to panic. Any overreaction on your part is only going to make it that much more difficult to be a successful parent. Instead you have to remain calm, methodical, and vigilant.

The role of parent isn't one that ends suddenly. It's not a race to the finish line because there is no ending. Once that first baby is born, you become a parent forever. And whether your child keeps you up at night because he's teething, or because it's midnight and he's not home yet, or because your daughter is in the hospital pushing out your first grandchild: it all comes under the same category, parenting. But you are not only a parent, you're also an individual, a spouse, an employee and who knows what other hats you wear. So if you're a parent, you're automatically also a juggler. Now every once in a while you're going to drop one of those balls. There's no avoiding it. And when that happens, you have to run after it and just start juggling again. However, if you're always worried about dropping a ball, the very act of worrying is going to distract you sufficiently to drop even more balls. In order to be a good juggler, you have to do it as effortlessly as possible. Understanding that paradox is the key to being a successful parent.

It's not that you don't have to sweat the details, because you do. You do have to keep up with all the latest dangers sweeping across the Internet aimed at your children, but you have to do it without becoming obsessed over it. If you're breathing down your children's necks all the time, then instead of obeying you, they're going to look for ways to break free, which will open them up to the very dangers from which you're trying to protect them. For your children to grow up to be successful adults, part of your job is to be the one to instigate their risk taking while at the same time trying to mitigate the dangers from those risks. It's that balancing act that makes both tasks that much harder. But just as juggling is relatively easy once you get the hang of it, parenting is relatively simple if you follow some basic rules: Maintain the lines of communication open between you and your partner so that you parent as a team. Keep up with the latest news by reading books like this one and keeping an eye on media for information and stories that apply to children so that even if you can't stay one step ahead of your children at least they won't be able to get so far ahead that they're out of your sight. Talk to other parents to learn from their experiences. And use plain old common sense.

And while you're doing all that, I want you to also be making sure that you're having the best sex possible!

MySpace Contract

The contract on the following page regarding computer use has been put out by MySpace. Whether you use this one, or change it somewhat, or make up an entirely new one, the idea is to put down on paper the rules and regulations you and your spouse feel are necessary to protect your children. That's an important point to make when discussing this contract. You're not enforcing arbitrary rules but instead are fulfilling your role as parents in keeping your children safe.

The advantage of putting these rules down on paper is that later on your child cannot say that they either did not know or did not understand the rules. I would recommend that you force your children to read the rules out loud to you so that you can be 100% sure that they read them at least once. And there's nothing wrong with bringing them out once in a while as a refresher.

As children grow older, the rules may be altered. There's nothing wrong with that. Teens develop more and more rights with every passing year. But just because you may one day change the rules doesn't mean that they're not enforceable under current conditions, and this contract has a place to put down what the consequences of breaking the rules will be.

FAMILY INTERNET SAFETY RULES AND USAGE CONTRACT

Kids, before you get started read these 3 statements out loud and initial them.

1. Nothing on the Internet is private. ____
2. People online are not always who they say they are.____
3. People are not always truthful online.____

I _____ agree on this date ___/___/___ to:

- Never give out our last name, address, phone number, or any personal information without parental consent.
  This includes the name of my school, where I play sports, the names of my family members, and anything else included below:

- Additional "Never give out rules":_____
  _____

- Never give out my password to anyone other than my parents.

- Always let my parents review existing and new screen names, e-mail addresses, user logins, and all passwords.

- Get my parents' permission before I sign up for anything on the Internet.

- Never upload or download pictures without parental consent.

- Never download games, music, or videos without parental consent. (Many viruses infect your computer this way.)

- When asked where we live, we all agree to say this online:
  _____
  Examples: (can't give out this info, the moon, state, OZ, N/A.)

- Never order anything online, even if it says "free," without parental consent.
  (Remember, nothing is free, some places just want your e-mail address so they can bombard you with spam, i.e., garbage e-mail.)

- Stop what I am doing and immediately get my parents or an adult I trust if someone asks to meet me in person.
  (*This is a very serious matter and is NOT to be taken lightly.)

- Stop communicating with someone if the conversation gets uncomfortable or if crude or inappropriate language is used.

- Never give out my age or any of my family's or friends' ages online.

- Never use inappropriate language online.

- Never click on a popup banner or sign. (Always click on the X on the top right corner to close them.)

- Report a bully immediately to my parents and never bully someone else.

- Never enter a site that states "you must be 18 to enter."

- Limit my time on the Internet to: _____ a day, homework is excluded here.

The adults agree:

If my child comes and tells me that they saw something online that was inappropriate, I will discuss this openly with him or her.

If my child reports a violation, I will discuss the matter with him or her first before calling the contract broken.

If this contract is broken the consequences will be:

_____

_____

_____

_____

I agree to abide by this contract.

Parents' signature: _____

Kid's signature: _____

Signed on ___/___/___

Web Resources

http://www.cdc.gov/std/default/htm—If you have any questions about any sexually transmitted diseases, this is one site where you can get correct information.

http://www.connectsafely.org—This site has information and a good forum where parents and teens can get information from each other.

http://www.ed.gov/pubs/parents/internet/index.html—This site is provided by the U.S. Dept of Education and has a booklet for parents called The Parents Guide to the Internet. I'm sorry to report that the date on it is 1997, so while there is some useful information, it's far from up-to-date.

http://www.filterreview.com—This site offers reviews of 20 filtering programs; however you have to submit information, including your e-mail address, to use it.

http://www.getnetwise.org—This is another excellent site. You can find detailed lists of all the software filtering tools available. This site covers a lot more than just keeping your children safe, and can get a little technical, but it is also very thorough.

http://www.goaskalice.columbia.edu/—This long-running site answers questions of interest to teens about sex, drinking, drugs, fitness and nutrition, relationships, and other areas. While it's a no-holds-barred site, the answers are all scientifically and medically correct.

http://www.ikeepsafe.org—This site is for children rather than teens, and has a cartoon mascot that helps teach kids about safety on the Internet. It was formed by a coalition of leading technological companies, like AOL and Dell, and is affiliated with a long list of organizations. If you have any younger children, this would be a good site to explore together.

http://monitoring-software-review.toptenreviews.com—This site provides reviews of monitoring software, including where to get the best price. It has useful if limited information.

http://www.netsmartz411.org—This site from the National Center for Missing and Exploited Children is well made and chock full of information for both parents, teens, and younger children. It's well worth exploring. There are simple step-by-step explanations on how to check out what your child is doing on the Internet.

http://www.onguardonline.gov—"OnGuardOnline.gov provides practical tips from the federal government and the technology industry to help you be on guard against Internet fraud, secure your computer, and protect your personal information" (home page). While this site is aimed at adults, you can find some good information that will also help you protect your teens.

http://www.plannedparenthood.org/—The Planned Parenthood site will give you accurate information on every form of birth control, as well as on sexually transmitted diseases and pretty much any other subject having to deal with sex that a teen, or parent, might need. There's even a gynecologist available to answer questions on a wide variety of subject matter.

http://www.safesurf.com—Other sites can rate themselves on this site and then use the site's logo to let people know whether or not a site is safe for children. Part of the reason this site was created was to avoid government censorship. You can download a free program that allows you to decide at what level of safety your browser will connect to sites. While this system is good as far as it goes, that is to say with sites that have self-rated themselves as appropriate or not, it won't protect your children from sites that are unrated.
http://www.safeteens.com—This site doesn't have a lot of bells and whistles, but the information for both parents and teens is easily accessible.

http://www.sexetc.org—"*Sex, Etc.* is an award-winning national magazine and Web site on sexual health that is written by teens, for teens.

It is part of the Teen-to-Teen Sexuality Education Project developed by Answer (formerly the Network for Family Life Education), a leading national organization dedicated to providing and promoting comprehensive sexuality education. Answer is part of the Center for Applied Psychology at Rutgers, The State University of New Jersey" (About Us).

http://www.surfswellisland.org—This site is for children and was put together by Disney. The home page has commercials from major companies, so rather than a public service, it seems to be a commercial venture. There's nothing wrong with that, but it's the exception rather than the rule among the sites aimed at promoting Web safety.

http://www.teenangels.com—This is a sister site of WiredSafety. org. This organization is comprised of volunteer teens who've been trained in cyber safety and who give lectures at schools and events on this topic.

http://www.teenpregnancy.org—National Campaign to Prevent Teen Pregnancy. This site contains good information, is constantly kept up to date, and doesn't talk down to teens because much of the content is produced by teens. It also contains thoughtful material for parents. You'll learn a lot from checking out this site.

http://www.teensource.org—"TeenSource.org, is an educational Web site launched in July 2001 by the California Family Health Council, Inc. (CFHC) as a resource for teens and young adults between the ages of 13 and 24 seeking information on healthy and responsible sexual lifestyles. CFHC is a nonprofit organization striving to improve the health of Californians by ensuring access to quality, comprehensive reproductive health and family planning services" (About Us).

http://www.wiredsafety.org—"WiredSafety provides help, information and education to Internet and mobile device users of all ages. [Help is offered for] victims of cyberabuse ranging from online fraud, cyberstalking and child safety, to hacking and malicious code attacks" (home page). The site also helps parents with issues such as MySpace and cyberbullying. You can also find speakers for schools. This is an excellent site for learning about the dangers because it is thorough but also acknowledges that teens need to use computers and can do so safely.

About the Authors

Born in Germany in 1928, **Dr. Ruth K. Westheimer** is an internationally renowned sex therapist and pioneer in media psychology. After emigrating to the United States in 1956, she obtained her Masters Degree in Sociology from the Graduate Faculty of the New School of Social Research. In 1970, she received a Doctorate of Education (Ed.D.) in the Interdisciplinary Study of the Family from Teachers College, Columbia University. The success of her radio program *Sexually Speaking,* which began in 1980 on WYNY-FM in New York, prompted the growth of a communications network that currently distributes Dr. Westheimer's expertise through television, books, newspapers, games, home video, computer software, and her own website, www.drruth.com.

Currently Dr. Westheimer is an Adjunct Professor at NYU, an Associate Fellow of Calhoun College at Yale University, and a Fellow of Butler College at Princeton University. In addition to having her own private practice, she frequently lectures at universities across the country and has twice been named "College Lecturer of the Year."

Over the past 20 years, **Pierre A. Lehu** has collaborated on numerous books with Dr. Ruth, including *52 Lessons on Communicating Love, Dr. Ruth's Sex After 50,* and *Sex for Dummies.*